ANTHROPOLOGY IN USE

A Bibliographic Chronology
of the Development
of Applied Anthropology

John van Willigen
Department of Anthropology
Applied Anthropology Documentation Project
Margaret I. King Library

University of Kentucky

Redgrave Publishing Company

Copyright © 1980 by
Redgrave Publishing Company
430 Manville Road
Pleasantville, New York 10570

All rights reserved. No portion of this book may be reproduced by any process or technique, without the formal consent of the publisher.

ISBN: 0-913178-66-7

Printed in the United States of America

REDGRAVE PUBLISHING COMPANY
P.O. BOX 67
SOUTH SALEM, NY 10590

CONTENTS

Introduction   Pages 1-8

   The Nature of Applied Anthropology
      Role
      Values
      Conceptualization
      Domain of Application
   A Brief History of Applied Anthropology
   Factors Relating to Career Choice
   The Structure of the Bibliography

Bibliographic Chronology   Entries 1-332

Indexes
   General
   Geographic

Introduction

The initial motivation to prepare this bibliography came from my experiences teaching Anthropology 525, "Applied Anthropology," at the University of Kentucky. Through that course I began to discover something of the diversity of anthropologists' experiences in problem solving throughout the history of the discipline. I also learned that these experiences were poorly documented and largely unavailable as training materials. Further, these early cases are ignored in significant proportion by practicing applied anthropologists and were not collected for purposes of documentation. These conditions suggested a need to improve the overall level of documentation in applied anthropology. Working with limited resources, this need has been addressed by the creation of the Special Collections Division of the Applied Anthropology Documentation Project at the Margaret I. King Library of the University of Kentucky. The Project has engaged the problem of collecting and organizing an archive of the written materials produced by practicing applied anthropologists in the course of their work. This project, which has the sponsorship of the Society for Applied Anthropology, served as a basis for this version of the bibliography.

Specifically, this bibliography is intended to meet two needs. First, it is intended to improve access to existing case studies for practicing applied anthropologists who may find activities which parallel their own among them. Second, it is intended to depict schematically the history of applied anthropology with reference to materials which may allow further study. The reader can judge whether or not either need is met.

This introduction will consider the nature of applied anthropology, its history, current factors affecting career choices in applied anthropology, and the structure of this bibliography.

The Nature of Applied Anthropology

Applied anthropology can be conveniently defined as "anthropology put to use." This definition is a useful starting point, but it is insufficiently concrete to be a meaningful guide to discussion.

As the reader reviews the content of the bibliography he or she will discover the breadth of the subfield. It is clear that there are many varieties of applied anthropology. Further, the differences between these types are significant from the standpoint of training and practice. The differences which appear to be the most important are summarized below.

2 ANTHROPOLOGY IN USE

Role

Applied anthropologists vary significantly in the range of activities which they accept as part of their role. The traditional core consists of the interrelated roles of teacher, researcher and expert. Some applied anthropologists have come to extend their role beyond this to include the activities of planner, innovator, culture broker, administrator, policy maker, change agent, and evaluator. All these new activities continue to involve the traditional core roles. Role extension in applied anthropology seems to have been carried furthest by North Americans and most dramatically in the period immediately following the Second World War. It occurred first in research and development anthropology, action anthropology, and the pioneering action research approaches. These extended-role approaches were later supplemented by community development, cultural brokerage, and community advocacy anthropology.

Values

Variability in value orientation runs parallel to variability in roles. That is, as applied anthropologists engaged a wider range of roles it became necessary for them to modify the "value-free, relativistic position of the anthropological researcher. The period after World War II frequently saw applied anthropologists explicitly using values as guides for action. In the research and development approach to application, for example, value categories are the basis for the entire development effort. Anthropologists using this technique plan their programs to increase the extent and breadth of sharing of certain human values such as power, wealth, enlightenment, etc.

All value-explicit approaches in some way involve intervention. Applied anthropology could theoretically be divided into two large categories: one limited to research and teaching, and the other involving research and teaching but extended to include intervention. It should be noted that current growth in applied anthropology is not occurring in the intervention realm, but in various areas of specialized policy research such as social impact assessment and evaluation.

Conceptualization

Much application of anthropology is done without an explicit conceptualized approach or method of application. It is assumed that a great number of applications will continue to be carried out in this way. A reader of the bibliography will be able to develop an understanding of the various approaches if they review some of the listed readings.

Domain of Application

It should be noted, finally, that a major variable influencing the shape of application is the context within which anthropology is put to use. A review of the bibliography will reveal the increasing range of areas of application. It should be noted that much of the growth in the range of research topics in disciplinary anthropology comes as a derivative of previous attempts at policy research. Research into health, land tenure, law, migration, urban life, nutrition, religious movements and others seem often to have occurred first in the applied realm, and later to have been adopted by purely academic researchers as a legitimate topic.

We started this discussion with a common sense definition of applied anthropology as simply anthropological knowledge and methods put to use. This definition ignores most of the variation in practice, and it also fails to resolve important conceptual problems in applied anthropology. One of these is the relationship between research and intervention. Some applied anthropologists confine themselves to research activities, even to the point of excluding the possibility of direct involvement in intervention. In this bibliography, however, applied anthropology can often be seen as a combination of research and intervention, although among applied anthropologists we find specialists in both policy researchers and intervention. Because of this reality, I have chosen to define applied anthropology as a complex of related, research-based, instrumental activities which produce socially desired change or stability in specific cultural systems through the provision of data, the initiation of direct action and/or the formulation of policy.

A Brief History of Applied Anthropology

Applied anthropologists seem to have generally poor comprehension of the history of the field, yet one must agree with George Foster's comment that the "current forms and place (of applied anthropology) within the broad discipline can be fully appreciated only with knowledge of the several stages of its development" (1969: 181). But applied anthropology has proceeded without a highly focused direction or clearly understood course of previous development. Without understanding our history we will, with apologies to Santayana and Karl Heider, be lucky enough to repeat it. That is, we have learned very little from our successes or our failures.

4 ANTHROPOLOGY IN USE

The history of applied anthropology and anthropology proper seem to be of roughly equal lengths; that is, the applied and non-applied portions of the discipline developed in parallel. Frequently the earliest professional anthropologists were engaged in research or instruction which was motivated by policy questions. Applied anthropology and anthropology proper influenced each other. This may seem like an obvious statement but in fact, commentaries on the nature of the relationship between the two categories often overlook the contribution of applied anthropology to the field in general. The most striking contribution is that anthropologists seeking data which addressed policy problems often led the way into new areas of inquiry. This pattern of adaptive-radiation continues to the present. Although it is more difficult to illustrate, various anthropologists have asserted that through use anthropological knowledge is tested and improved. This suggests that applied anthropology has improved the quality of anthropology proper.

The history of applied anthropology can be depicted in three eras. These are: the predisciplinary period, which ends in 1860 and has no specified beginning; the research-consultant period, which covers the period between 1860 and 1941, and the role-extension period, which encompasses 1941 to the present.

The predisciplinary period consists of a small number of documented cases in which persons use cultural knowledge to engage a practical problem and attempt to solve it. (See entries 1, 2, 3, 7, 9. Henceforth, relevant entries will be shown in parentheses). This area also is characterized by the creation of early associations of people concerned with the use of cultural knowledge (5) and early policy research projects (4, 6).

The research consultant period is named after the most prevalent activity in the period. Its beginning is marked by the identification of anthropology as a distinct discipline, and its end by the emergence of applied anthropology as a separate branch of the discipline manifested by the founding of the Society for Applied Anthropology (93).

During this period the first academic programs in anthropology were developed (13) and numerous policy research organizations were created which hired anthropologists (11, 17, 18, 20, 25, 28, 46, 54, 75, 78). Anthropologists were frequently hired to serve various purposes in government (29, 34, 38, 41, 45, 47, 48, 55, 61, 77, 84). Numerous cases of administrative trouble-shooting in cross-cultural settings are to be found. The most striking are James Mooney's work with the Ghost Dance among the Sioux (16); W. S. Rattray's work among the Ashanti (43); and F. E. Williams's work concerning New Guinea cargo-cults (47). Another frequent use of anthropologists is the training of colonial administrators. Early examples are found in the Netherlands (9, 40), France (15), South Africa (24, 37), Great Britain (30), Belgium (39), and New Guinea (49, 51). Perhaps the most interesting of the activities which emerge during this period are special purpose policy research groups which were set up by various governments. Among the earliest were the Direccion of Anthropology established by the Mexican government at the time of the Revolution (35) and the Institute of Ethnography established by the government of the Soviet Union (36). Later a number of applied research groups were established in the United States. These include the Rio Grande Socio-economic Survey of the United States Department of Agriculture (68), the applied Anthropology Unit of the Bureau of Indian Affairs (70), the Technical Cooperation-Bureau of Indian Affairs group (72), the Rural Life Studies of the United States Department of Agriculture (86), the Committee for National Morale (83), and the Committee on Food Habits (87).

While this period saw a dramatic expansion into new topical areas, the role of the applied anthropologist remained quite limited in scope. That is, applied anthropologists limited their role activities to that of researcher and teacher. The typical applied anthropologist of this period worked as a research or training consultant in government on private sector development activities. They rarely activated a central role in decision making. It is during the next period that we see an increase in the number of action-involved roles activated by anthropologists. This shift is referred to in the name given this period; that is, the period of role extension.

Clearly World War II dramatically changed applied anthropology. In both the United States and Britain, anthropologists were involved in the war effort. The American Anthropological Association passed a resolution pledging anthropological support in the war effort (90). Many American anthropologists came to work for the War Relocation Authority (91, 95). Others worked on research which was to identify the psychocultural nature of both enemy and allies (99, 106) or to prepare technical background on areas in anticipation of postwar administration (107). The war seemed to accelerate trends toward more intense involvement already at work which formed during "New Deal" times.

In North American applied anthropology, new patterns of practice begin to emerge as early as 1941. An early example is Laura Thompson's use of action research techniques to help improve American Indian administration (94). Constructive attempts to improve the public health status of American Indians also occurred (105).

The development by anthropologists of action-involved, extended role approaches for social intervention began to occur

6 ANTHROPOLOGY IN USE

shortly after the war. The first of these is action anthropology, (133) developed by Sol Tax and his associates. Action anthropology had both development and research goals. Research and development anthropology was developed a few years later by Allen Holmberg (168). Research and development involved the use of a sophisticated conception of values coupled with economic educational and political interventions. Action anthropology was used in some other contexts, including urban Chicago (170), pan-Indian leadership (202), Chicano education (240), and Cheyenne religious revival (261). Research and development anthropology was replicated in a number of settings in Peru (198), as well as in Los Angeles (282) and southern Utah (290).

At about the same time that both action anthropology and research and development anthropology developed, anthropologists were beginning to contribute to the so-called community development movement. This contribution included consultation on program development (138), evaluation (164, 187), development of training materials (186, 210, 218), and administration (231, 243).

Other approaches for applying anthropological knowledge were developed later. An approach called "Action Research" was developed by Stephen Schensul in the late 1960s (244). This approach was to be rooted in the first generation techniques, such as action anthropology, and was an adaption to big city ethnic politics.

The other significant second generation approach to applying anthropological knowledge is cultural brokerage. Hazel Weidman developed this technique to improve the functioning of the health care system of Dade County, Florida. She, it should be noted, does not regard this approach as a kind of applied anthropology (259).

Other than the development of these approaches, the most significant events during this period are the various legislative acts which stimulated research efforts among anthropologists. Of course many of these were passed quite a while ago, but they continue to have their effects. Relevant legislation which influenced work opportunities for anthropologists includes the Antiquities Act of 1906 (26), the Historic Sites Act of 1935 (69), the Indian Reorganization Act of 1934 (70), the Colonial Development and Welfare Act of 1940 (89), the Indian Claims Commission Act of 1946 (104, 122, 166, 181), the Peace Corps Act of 1961 (208, 228), the Economic Opportunity Act of 1964 (233, 238), the National Environmental Policy Act of 1969 (248, 274, 277, 292, 294, 305), the Foreign Assistance Act as amended in 1973 (283, 316) and the Community Development Act of 1974 (292).

It is very important to note that during the period of role-extension, applied anthropologists continued to perform much the same kinds of research and consulting activities which they had carried on previously. This included research on various policy-relevant topics such as agriculture (195, 256, 304, 307, 309), alcoholism (241), bilingual education (314, 320), business administration (124, 266, 280), communication (175), community health (161, 209, 286, 303), drug use (245), employment (97, 110, 262, 299), and ethnic relations (88). Also appearing are genocide (322), housing (252, 287), land use (92, 104, 114, 121, 122), law (98), migration (130, 142), nutrition (87), population studies (193, 213, 271), sanitation (313), and welfare reform (311).

The future of applied anthropology will be characterized by even greater diversity. One can only guess about the content of future versions of this bibliography. It seems clear, however, that the shape of the field will be formed by both the challenges created by forces outside the discipline and the strength and quality of the adaptations of individual anthropologists and the relevant associations. The importance of external factors must be understood. The most important factor is the realities of the academic job market. These factors are considered in the next section.

Factors Relating to Career Choice

As most anthropologists are aware, there is increasing interest in the realm of application within the discipline. While there are both "push" and "pull" factors, the push factors seem more often to be discussed publicly. The most important factor pushing anthropologists toward nonacademic or applied careers is the limited growth in academic positions. The problem is most clearly reported in an article entitled "Academic Opportunity in Anthropology, 1974-90," by R. G. D'Andrade, E. A. Hammel, D. L. Adkins, and C. K. McDaniel, published in the *American Anthropologist* in 1975 (299). That is, because of a decline in the birth rate there will be a significant decrease in the number of college age Americans for the foreseeable future. This demographic fact will result in a significant decrease in the number of academic positions available to anthropologists. The decline in college age students is coupled with an increase in the number of anthropologists receiving graduate degrees. While our problem is not a unique one, the quest for a solution will have to occur at the level of the discipline.

One of the responses to our problem has been to place increased emphasis upon the nonacademic career. This seems

8 ANTHROPOLOGY IN USE

inevitable, given the prediction of D'Andrade et al.: "Our most optimistic assessment of the future of academic employment in anthropology indicates that after 1982 over two-thirds of all anthropology Ph.D.'s will have to find employment outside academia" (299). Increasingly anthropology departments are beginning to gear up to prepare their students for nonacademic careers. The American Anthropological Association has begun to manifest concern for the needs of nonacademically employed anthropologists through its Committee on Anthropology as a Profession. Local associations of anthropologists orientated toward application and toward nonacademic employment have been organized.

This concern has resulted in an increase in intensity of debate concerning such questions as "What is applied anthropology?" "What should the role of the applied anthropologist be?" and "What is the potential contribution of anthropology as a policy-relevant science?"

It is the purpose of this bibliography to provide a guide to the documents which can help answer the above questions.

The Structure of the Bibliography

The bibliography attempts to document events in the history of applied anthropology, including:

1. early uses by "proto-anthropologists" of cultural knowledge for some policy purpose.

2. early appointments of anthropologists in various policy or administrative positions.

3. projects which demonstrated the utility of specific modes for applying anthropology.

4. the publication of books important for training applied anthropologists or others who would use anthropology for some practical purpose.

5. the passage of legislation which had a direct effect on the work opportunities of anthropologists.

6. the formation of associations and institutes which primarily work with aspects of applied anthropology.

7. research projects which were carried out with the intent of having a direct impact on policy, administration, or litigation.

8. the development of training programs in anthropology for government officials.

Each component of the chronology consists of a brief statement describing an event. These statements are coupled with one or more bibliographic citations which may be either descriptions or products of activities noted. Dates indicate only the starting point of activities. The activities are quite variable in their significance, but nevertheless may all be useful in developing an understanding of applied anthropology's history. The geographic location of the event is indicated by the terminology which was relevant at the time. In other words, a term such as Tanganyika would be used in place of the current name Tanzania. Geographic terms are almost always national, although occasionally larger geographic regions are used.

Two indexes are provided. These are a general index, which includes persons and subjects, and a geographic index. The general index includes persons referred to in the annotation as well as authors cited in the bibliography. Geographic location includes all nations referred to either in the headings or the text of each annotation.

It is difficult to assess the quality of the coverage of the bibliography in both time and space. The bibliography includes only those "events" which have come to be part of the written record in the form of journal articles, "news and notes" items, books, presented papers, historical surveys, and technical reports. It is clear that the written record of applied anthropology is neither easily accessible nor complete. These problems of accessibility are caused by the following:

A. The written materials produced as a direct result of the applied process are inappropriate to many existing publication outlets. Existing anthropology journals have been allocated largely to nonapplied publications. There are no journals which are exclusively dedicated to publishing applied anthropology on a timely basis. Reports written by applied anthropologists frequently have to be substantially rewritten in order to be suitable for journal publication.

B. Applied anthropologists may publish their materials in a wide variety of journals, thereby causing problems of bibliographic control.

C. Applied anthropologists are not highly motivated to publish, in contrast to academic anthropologists, because their salary increments and promotions are seldom tied to this activity.

The nonacademically employed applied anthropologists will frequently produce a lot of written material in the course of their work. Many of these "naturally occurring" documents are valuable as a means of understanding the sociocultural situation to which they are addressed and as depictions of problem-solving techniques. Yet for the most part these documents rarely are published and frequently become what has been termed "fugitive" literature. One can imagine how instructive it would be to have better access to all of the many technical reports, memos, and planning papers produced by anthropologists in the course of the application process.

The effects of these limitations in bibliographic access and control are striking. The field, though active, does not seem to be undergoing rapid conceptual or methodological development. It needs to be more cumulative yet lacks the mechanisms to do this. Further, anthropologists involved in training applied anthropologists have limited access to the "in-print" products of practicing applied anthropologists; thus the amount of relevant training materials available is very limited, producing conditions which impair the training process. What tend to be most available are the efforts of academically employed applied anthropologists. In response to this array of problems, the University of Kentucky has developed the Documentation Project noted above. The Applied Anthropology Documentation Project is based on the assumption that the specific information needs of nonacademically employed anthropologists are not being adequately met by existing library resources. The Project will collect materials produced by applied anthropologists in the course of their work. At this time the Project has accumulated a sizable collection of technical reports, conference papers, proposals, and manuscripts, but is actively seeking more materials. Readers who care to contribute materials to the Project may send them to: Applied Anthropology Documentation Project, Margaret I. King Library, Special Collections, University of Kentucky, Lexington, Kentucky 40506. Materials will be included in subsequent editions of this bibliography and the collection. The collection would benefit from the contribution of technical reports and other limited circulation documents, specifically such things as social impact assessment reports, evaluation studies, feasibility studies, technology assessments, and proposals relating to the same. Materials relating to the development of training in aspects of anthropology for various kinds of change agents, health care professionals, government officials, educators and the like would be most welcome. Documents relating to applied anthropology training programs are also sought.

BIBLIOGRAPHIC CHRONOLOGY 1-5

1   GREAT BRITAIN   596

Pope Gregory I made recommendations to his missionaries in Britain that the pagan temples not be destroyed so as to minimize conflict with the British tribals, and thereby facilitate conversion. Gregory also suggested that the pagan animal sacrifices be converted in terms of their meaning to feastdays honoring the saints.

Jeffereys, M. D. W.
1956   Some Rules of Directed Culture Change Under Roman Catholicism. American Anthropologist. 58:721-731.

2   CONGO   1682

The Capuchin priest and missionary to the Congo, Fr. Jerome Merolla da Sorrento developed various "policies" to increase the effectiveness of the mission program. One policy was to attempt to convert those who might be called today "opinion leaders" so as to accelerate conversion.

Jeffereys, M. D. W.
1956   Some Rules of Directed Culture Change Under Roman Catholicism. American Anthropologist. 58:721-731.

3   SPAIN   1766

One of Charles III's ministers, a certain unpopular Sicilian named Marquis de Squillaci attempted to prohibit various items of popular dress. This prohibition resulted in a crisis including the banishment of the King. Ultimately the goal of prohibition was achieved by making the items of dress the official "uniform of the public executioner."

Foster, George
1956   Applied Anthropology and Modern Life. In Estudios Antropologicos, publicados en homenaje al doctor Manuel Gamio. Mexico, D. F.

4   INDIA   1807

Dr. Francis Buchanan was appointed by the East India Company to study life and culture in Bengal.

Sachchidananda
1972   Planning, Development and Applied Anthropology in India. Journal of the Indian Anthropological Society. 7:11-28.

5   GREAT BRITAIN   1838

The Aborigines Protection Society, established in London, was concerned with both research and social service for the native population. A more academically oriented faction of the society

6–9 ANTHROPOLOGY IN USE

became formalized as the Ethnological Society of London in 1843.

Keith, Arthur
1971   How Can the Institute Best Serve the Needs of Anthropology? Journal of the Royal Anthropological Society. 47:12-30.

Reining, Conrad C.
1962   A Lost Period of Applied Anthropology. American Anthropologist. 64:593-600.

6   UNITED STATES   1852

Henry R. Schoolcraft, one of the founders of the American Ethnological Society was retained by the United States Congress to compile Information Respecting the History, Condition and Prospects of the Indian Tribes of the United States which was published in 1852. He was motivated by the idea that the information would lead to a more objective policy toward the native American.

Partridge, William L. and Elizabeth M. Eddy
1978   The Development of Applied Anthropology in America. In Applied Anthropology in America. Elizabeth M. Eddy and William L. Partridge (eds.), Columbia University Press: New York.

Schoolcraft, Henry R.
1852-57 Information Respecting the History, Condition, and Prospects of the Indian Tribes of the United States. 6 vols. Philadelphia, Pa.: Lippincott.

7   UNITED STATES   1860

William Duncan, a missionary, made efforts at social reform among Northwest Coast Indian groups. This is an early example of a culturally aware change agent.

Barnett, H. G.
1942   Applied Anthropology in 1860. Applied Anthropology. 1:19-32.

8   DENMARK   1862

Hinrich Rink was trained as a natural historian and served as an administrator. He contributed to the early development of self-determination among Greenland natives.

Nellemann, George
1969   Hinrich Rink and Applied Anthropology in Greenland in the 1860s. Human Organization. 28:166-174.

9   NETHERLANDS   1864

Ethnology was included in a training program for civil servants to

BIBLIOGRAPHIC CHRONOLOGY 10–13

serve in the Netherlands East Indies. The Netherlands was one of the first countries to make use of anthropology as part of colonial administration training.

Held, G. Jan
1953   Applied Anthropology in Government: The Netherlands. In Anthropology Today. A. L. Kroeber (ed.), Chicago: University of Chicago.

Kennedy, Raymond
1944   Applied Anthropology in the Dutch East Indies. Transactions of the New York Academy of Sciences. Ser. 2. VI:157-62.

10   GREAT BRITAIN   1866

The Anthropological Society of London began to publish the *Popular Magazine of Anthropology*. This periodical contained articles on applied topics. Many articles promoted the use of applied anthropology.

Reining, Conrad C.
1962   A Lost Period of Applied Anthropology. American Anthropologist. 64:593-600.

11   UNITED STATES   1879

The Bureau of American Ethnology was founded "to produce results that would be of practical value in the administration of Indian affairs." The BAE initially was involved in basic exploration. The term acculturation was first used in a BAE document.

Powell, John Wesley
1881   First Annual Report of the Bureau of Ethnology (1879-80). Washington, D.C.: Government Printing Office.

12   CAPE COLONY   1880

The government of Cape Colony established a "commission of enquiry" which examined the "customs and institutions of the native populations."

Myres, J. L.
1928   The Science of Man in the Service of the State. Journal of the Royal Anthropological Institute of Great Britain and Ireland. LIX:19-52.

13   GREAT BRITAIN   1883

E. B. Tylor received the first academic appointment in anthropology. Tylor was appointed Reader in Anthropology at Oxford.

Foster, George
1969   Applied Anthropology. Boston: Little, Brown and Company.

14–16 ANTHROPOLOGY IN USE

14 UNITED STATES   1885

   The Omaha Allotment Act, which was a pilot for the General Allotment
   Act of 1887 (The Dawes Act) was passed. Alice Fletcher, who served
   as alloting agent to the Omaha and other tribes, lobbied for both
   acts. The promotion of the act was based on certain basic under-
   standings of cultural dynamics, that is private ownership would lead
   to assimilation. The act proved a tragedy for Indians in spite of
   the planners' good intentions and the use of primitive culture change
   theory.

   Lurie, Nancy O.
   1966   Women in Early American Anthropology. In Pioneers of
            American Anthropology: the Uses of Biography. J. Helm
            (ed.), Seattle: University of Washington Press.

15 FRANCE   1889

   Ecole Nationale de la France D'Outre-Mer was founded to provide
   training for the colonial service. The school was an agency of
   the French government and offered training in the ethnology of
   Southeast Asia and Africa.

   Leroi-Gourhan, A.
   1953   France. In International Directory of Anthropological
            Institutions. William L. Thomas, Jr. and Anna Pikelis
            (eds.), New York: Wenner-Gren.

16 UNITED STATES   1891

   Anthony Wallace suggests that an early occurrence of a policy study
   in anthropology is James Mooney's The Ghost Dance Religion and the
   Sioux Outbreak of 1890. Mooney considered the causes of the pheno-
   menon. Hinsley questions whether Mooney was motivated by policy
   considerations.

   Mooney, James
   1896   The Ghost Dance Religion and the Sioux Outbreak of 1890.
            Fourteenth Annual Report. Washington: Bureau of American
            Ethnology.

   Hinsley, Curtis M., Jr.
   1979   Anthropology as Science and Politics: the Dilemmas of the
            Bureau of American Ethnology, 1879 to 1904. In The Uses
            of Anthropology. Walter Goldschmidt (ed.). (A special
            publication of the American Anthropological Association
            Number 11.) Washington, D.C.: American Anthropological
            Association.

   Wallace, Anthony F. C.
   1976   Some Reflections on the Contributions of Anthropologists
            to Public Policy. In Anthropology and the Public Interest,
            Fieldwork and Theory. Peggy Reeves Sanday (ed.), New
            York: Academic Press.

BIBLIOGRAPHIC CHRONOLOGY 17–20

17   GREAT BRITAIN   1892

      The Ethnographic Survey of the United Kingdom, sponsored by a number of learned societies, was initiated.

      Myres, J. L.
      1928   The Science of Man in the Service of the State. Journal of the Royal Anthropological Institute of Great Britain and Ireland. LIX:19-52.

18   IRELAND   1893

      The Ethnographic Survey of Ireland was reported for the first time. This activity was sponsored by the Royal Irish Academy.

      Haddon, A. C.
      1897   The Study of Man. London: J. Murray.

19   UNITED STATES   1899

      Charles C. Royce's comprehensive study entitled <u>Indian Land Cessions in the United States</u> was published by the Bureau of American Ethnology. Hinsley cites this as a, "continuation of Powell's earlier involvement in Indian policy" at the Bureau. He also suggests that it marks the, "withdrawal from public concerns" of the Bureau.

      Hinsley, Curtis M., Jr.
      1979   Anthropology as Science and Politics: the Dilemmas of the Bureau of American Ethnology, 1879 to 1904. In The Uses of Anthropology. Walter Goldschmidt (ed.). (A special publication of the American Anthropological Association, Number 11.) Washington, D.C.: American Anthropological Association.

20   PHILIPPINES   1901

      David P. Barrows along with Merton L. Miller and Albert Jenks organized the Bureau of Non-Christian Tribes. Barrows was named its first Chief. Barrows strongly emphasized the importance of sound ethnology as the basis for effective administration. In addition he visited the United States to determine if the reservation system would be applicable to the Philippines.

      Eggan, Fred
      1974   Applied Anthropology in the Mountain Province, Philippines. In Social Organization and the Applications of Anthropology, Essays in Honor of Lauriston Sharp. Robert J. Smith (ed.). Ithaca: Cornell University Press.

      Barrows, David P.
      1902   Report of the Bureau of Non-Christian Tribes of the Philippine Islands for the Year Ended August 31, 1902. Washington, D.C.: Philippine Commission, Bureau of Insular Affairs, War Department.

21-24 ANTHROPOLOGY IN USE

21 UNITED STATES 1902

    The 1902 Annual Report of the Bureau of American Ethnology contained a proposal for what W. J. McGee called applied ethnology. This appeared to be an attempt to reemphasize the policy research mission of the Bureau at a time when it was involved in a crisis brought about by J. W. Powell's death and a financial scandal involving a minor employee. McGee's prospectus for applied ethnology proposed various kinds of policy studies focused on the United States and its colonial possessions. W. J. McGee was actually a geologist like Powell but assumed the title Ethnologist-in-Charge in 1893. McGee was committed to the applied role of ethnology.

Hinsley, Curtis M., Jr.
1976   Amateurs and Professionals in Washington Anthropology, 1879 to 1903. In American Anthropology, the Early Years. John V. Murra (ed.). 1974 Proceedings of the American Ethnological Society. New York: West Publishing Co.

22 PHILIPPINES 1903

    William Howard Taft, then Governor-General of the Philippines, appointed David P. Barrows as General Superintendent of Education for the Philippines.

Eggan, Fred
1974   Applied Anthropology in the Mountain Province, Philippines. In Social Organization and the Applications of Anthropology, Essays in Honor of Lauriston Sharp. Robert J. Smith (ed.). Ithaca: Cornell University Press.

23 GREAT BRITAIN 1904

    Much of the early development of academic anthropology in Great Britain was based upon the justification of potential application. In addition many early faculty were in fact ex-colonial administrators. At Cambridge, what Fortes calls the "first inaugural lecture" on anthropology was given by Sir Richard Temple who was ex-Indian Civil Service. Other early faculty were T. C. Hodson and J. H. Hutton, both ex-civil servants.

Fortes, Meyer
1953   Social Anthropology at Cambridge Since 1900. Cambridge: Cambridge University Press.

24 SOUTH AFRICA 1905

    A government inquiry into native affairs suggested that university positions be made available for teaching and ethnological research.

Forde, E. Daryll
1953   Applied Anthropology in Government: British Africa. In Anthropology Today. A. L. Kroeber (ed.). Chicago: University of Chicago Press.

BIBLIOGRAPHIC CHRONOLOGY 25–27

25 INDIA   1905

       Ethnographic Survey of India was initiated with H. H. Risley as its first director. The survey resulted in a series of basic ethnographies.

       Majumdar, D. N.
       1953   India, Pakistan, and Ceylon. In International Directory of Anthropological Institutions. William L. Thomas, Jr. and Anna M. Pikelis (eds.). New York: Wenner-Gren.

26 UNITED STATES   1906

       The Antiquities Act of 1906 (Public Law 59-209) was passed, providing for the protection of all historic and prehistoric ruins or monuments on federal lands. It prohibited the excavation or destruction of such antiquities without permission from the Secretaries of Interior, Agriculture, and Defense and limited permission to reputable institutions and museums seeking to preserve or increase knowledge of the remains. This Act further authorized the President to declare areas of public lands as national monuments and to reserve land for that purpose. This represented the first large scale involvement of the U.S. Government in cultural resource management.

       McGimsey, Charles R., III
       1973   Archaeology and Archaeological Resources. Washington, D.C.: Society for American Archaeology.

27 ITALY   1906

       Maria Montessori, trained as a physician and physical anthropologist, initiated a school for young children of low-income Roman families. The school made use of what was ultimately called the Montessori Method. The diffusion of the Montessori innovation in the United States is closely related to the foundation of the American Montessori Society in the early 1960s. A primary influence of anthropology on Montessori education can be seen in the role of the teacher, who is responsible for observing and recording much like an ethnographer. The view that each child has unique growth potential is consistent with the concept of cultural relativity. Error is permitted as an essential part of growth and learning in the Montessori classroom.

       Kramer, Rita
       1976   Maria Montessori: A Biography. New York: G. P. Putnam.

       Montessori, Maria
       1955   Childhood Education. New York: A Meridian Book.

       1964   The Montessori Method. New York: Schocken Books.

       1967   The Absorbent Mind. New York: A Dell Book.

       1973   From Childhood to Adolescence. New York: Schocken Books.

28-32 ANTHROPOLOGY IN USE

28   PHILIPPINES   1906

The Philippine Ethnological Survey, patterned after the surveys of the Bureau of American Ethnology, was active for four years. The project was directed by the American anthropologist, Albert E. Jenks. Jenks later developed applied anthropology programs at the University of Minnesota.

Kennard, Edward A. and Gordon MacGregor
1953   Applied Anthropology in Government: United States. In Anthropology Today. A. L. Kroeber (ed.). Chicago: University of Chicago Press.

29   NIGERIA   1906

The first government anthropologist appointed in Africa was W. Northcote Thomas. He served in Nigeria and later in Sierra Leone. Thomas' appointment was precipitated by a crisis concerning the applicability of indirect rule policies to the Ibo.

Lackner, Helen
1973   Social Anthropology and Indirect Rule. The Colonial Administration and Anthropology in Eastern Nigeria: 1920-1940. In Anthropology and the Colonial Encounter. Talal Asad (ed.). New York: Humanities Press.

30   GREAT BRITAIN   1908

Sir Reginald Wingate requested Oxford and Cambridge to offer anthropology as part of a training curriculum for civil servants being posted to the Sudan. Because of its status as a condominium of Great Britain and Egypt, the Sudan was administered by the Foreign Office rather than the Colonial Office. This seems to be related to earlier and more intensive use of anthropologists in government service there.

Myres, J. L.
1928   The Science of Man in the Service of the State. Journal of the Royal Anthropological Institute of Great Britain and Ireland. LIX:19-52.

31   SUDAN   1908

C. G. Seligman was hired to survey the Sudan ethnographically.

Seligman, C. G.
1932   Pagan Tribes of the Nilotic Sudan. London.

32   UNITED STATES   1909

Warren K. Moorehead, an archaeologist from Phillips Academy was appointed by President Theodore Roosevelt to the Board of Indian Commissioners. He remained on the board until it was dissolved in 1933.

BIBLIOGRAPHIC CHRONOLOGY 33-35

Stewart, Omer C.
1961 Kroeber and the Indian Claims Commission Cases. Alfred L. Kroeber: A Memorial. Kroeber Anthropological Society Papers. No. 25 (Fall).

33 UNITED STATES   1910

Franz Boas, the intellectual father of a generation of the very best American anthropologists was not an applied anthropologist but did, among the wide array of researches that he carried out, engage in policy significant research. The most significant of these was Boas' studies of the morphological changes in the New York City immigrant population. He found that there was a great deal of change in the stature of the immigrant populations intergenerationally. The research was published by the United States Immigration Commission. The results contradicted a number of racist ideas which suggested that the gene flow between the immigrant population and the "in-place" population would have a negative outcome. Boas was, of course, a committed anti-racist.

Boas, Franz
1910 Changes in Bodily Form of Descendents of Immigrants. Partial Report on the results of an anthropological investigation for the U.S. Immigration Commission. Washington, D.C.: Government Printing Office (Senate Document No. 208, 61st Congress, 2nd Session).

Stocking, George W., Jr.
1968 Race, Culture and Evolution: Essays in the History of Anthropology. New York: Free Press.

34 TONGA   1916

A. R. Radcliffe-Brown was appointed Director of Education of the Kingdom of Tonga. He served in this position until 1919.

Fortes, Meyer
1949 Preface. In Social Structure; Studies Presented to A. R. Radcliffe-Brown. M. Fortes (ed.). London: Oxford University Press.

35 MEXICO   1917

The revolutionary government of Mexico created the Direccion de Anthropologia within the Department of Agriculture and Development. Headed by Manuel Gamio, this organization is presented by Edward H. Spicer as the first manifestation of applied anthropology. While this organization lasted only until 1924 it nevertheless, "was a powerful influence for the application of anthropology in Mexico" (Spicer 1977:117). Gamio's ideas came to be expressed in the book Forjando Patria which focused upon the process by which the various cultures of Mexico could be integrated.

36-38 ANTHROPOLOGY IN USE

Comas, Juan
1975   Manuel Gamio, Antologia. Universidad Nacional Autonoma de Mexico, Mexico.

Gamio, Manuel
1916   Forjando Patria. Pronacionalismo Porrua Hermanos: Mexico.

Spicer, Edward H.
1977   Early Applications of Anthropology in North America. In Perspectives on Anthropology, 1976. Anthony F. C. Wallace et. al. (eds.). Washington, D.C.: American Anthropological Association. (A special publication of the American Anthropological Association).

36 UNION OF SOVIET SOCIALIST REPUBLICS   1917

The October Revolution radically changed the nature of the development of ethnography in the Soviet Union. Following the Revolution state sponsorship increased resulting in the creation of the Institute of Ethnography of the USSR Academy of Sciences. According to Julian Bromley Soviet Ethnography was very closely tied to the goals of the Revolution. As he notes, "the tasks of Lenin's national policy and the need for radical changes in the life and culture of the formerly backward peoples called for a thorough research into the ethnic composition of the population and the national peculiarities of its culture" (1976:99). Thus virtually the entire Soviet ethnography apparatus was a kind of applied anthropology enterprise.

Bromley, Yu. V.
1976   Ethnographical Studies in the USSR 1965-1975. In Soviet Ethnography: Main Trends (Problems of the Contemporary World No. 42). Moscow: USSR Academy of Sciences.

37 SOUTH AFRICA   1920

A. R. Radcliffe-Brown established a School of African Studies organized around a new anthropology department at the University of Cape Town. There he had some impact on government thinking both through special "applied anthropology" courses he established for government administrators and through lectures he delivered. The role of the anthropologist, as he saw it, was to provide scientific appraisals of the situations faced by administrators and not to advocate policy.

Kuper, Adam
1973   Anthropologists and Anthropology, the British School, 1922-1972. London: Allen Lane.

38 GOLD COAST   1920

W. S. Rattray was appointed to the newly created post of Government Anthropologist.

BIBLIOGRAPHIC CHRONOLOGY 39-43

Kuper, Adam
1973   Anthropologists and Anthropology, the British School, 1922-1972. London: Allen Lane.

39   BELGIUM   1920

Institute of Universitaire des Territories d' Outre'Mer was created in Antwerp to train colonial administrators. This training included studies in ethnology.

Nicaise, Joseph
1960   Applied Anthropology in the Congo and Ruanda-Urandi. Human Organization. 19:112-117.

40   NETHERLANDS   1921

Colonial civil service training at the University of Leiden included training in the ethnology and customary law of Indonesia. The effect of this was that virtually all Dutch colonial administrators had ethnology training.

Josselin de Jong, P. E.
1960   Cultural Anthropology in the Netherlands. Higher Education and Research in the Netherlands. 4:3-16.

41   NIGERIA   1921

C. K. Meek was appointed census commissioner. Meek was an administrative officer who had received anthropological training. Meek's work resulted in the gathering of ethnographic data as part of Nigerian census operations.

Hailey, W. H.
1957   An African Survey: Revised 1956. London: Oxford University.

42   NEW GUINEA   1921

The anthropologist, W. P. Chinnery, was appointed labor administrator in a New Guinea copper mine. This represents an exceptionally early use of anthropology in an industrial setting. His primary goals were maintaining a healthy and stable work force.

Chinnery, W. P.
1933   Applied Anthropology in New Guinea. Report of the Twenty-First Meeting of the Australian and New Zealand Association for the Advancement of Science, Sydney, New South Wales: Australian and New Zealand Association for the Advancement of Science.

43   GOLD COAST   1921

The Golden Stool Incident occurred. Capt. W. S. Rattray, government anthropologist, investigated the cultural meaning of the Golden

Stool which had been the focus of conflict between the British and
the Ashanti of West Africa. The Stool was interpreted by the Ashanti
as a repository of the nation's soul, whereas the British assumed
the Stool was a symbol of royal authority. In response to their
assumptions the British attempted to obtain the Stool to solidify
their leadership. This led to armed and bloody conflict with the
Ashanti. Rattray suggested that the British view was wrong and that
they desist from attempting to obtain the Stool. This advice was
followed and had the proper ameliorative effect. This represents
a classic case of cross-cultural trouble-shooting.

Rattray, R. S.
1923   Ashanti. Oxford: Clarendon Press.

44   UNITED STATES   1921

Albert Jenks established an Americanization training course at the
University of Minnesota. Designed to facilitate the assimilating
of immigrant Americans, the course also provided professional
training on the techniques of Americanization. Based on the existing
anthropology curriculum, the course made use of experiential
learning modes as well as classroom instruction.

Jenks, Albert E.
1921   The Relation of Anthropology to Americanization. The
        Scientific Monthly. 12:240-245.

1921   The Practical Value of Anthropology to Our Nation.
        Science, n.s. Vol. LIII, No. 1363 (February 18, 1921)
        pp. 147-156.

45   NEW GUINEA   1921

The first government anthropologist, W. M. Strong, was appointed
by Sir J. H. P. Murray. Strong was trained in medicine. He was
succeeded by F. E. Williams.

Chinnery, W. P.
1933   Applied Anthropology in New Guinea. Report of the 21st
        Meeting of the Australian and New Zealand Association
        for the Advancement of Science. pp. 163-175.

46   GREAT BRITAIN   1921

The Anthropological Section of the British Association for the
Advancement of Science advocated the establishment of a center
to coordinate training in anthropology in service to the Empire.
This proposition was approved and a center was established at the
Royal Anthropological Institute. The unit was referred to as the
Joint Committee on Research and Training.

Myres, J. L.
1928   The Science of Man in the Service of the State. Journal
        of the Royal Anthropological Institute of Great Britain
        and Ireland. LIX:19-52.

47 NEW GUINEA   1922

F. E. Williams began his tenure as the Australian Government Anthropologist by doing a trouble-shooting study of a cargo-cult which developed in response to European-native contact. The anthropologist recommended that the government not intervene in the movement. This recommendation was followed and minimized violence and bloodshed.

Williams, F. E.
1923   The Vailala Madness and the Destruction of Native Ceremonies in the Gulf Division. Port Moresby: Territory of Papua. Anthropology Report No. 4.

1934   The Vailala Madness in Retrospect. Essays Presented to C. G. Seligman. Evans-Pritchard, Firth, Malinowski and Schapera (eds.). London: Kegan Paul, French, Trubner.

48 NEW GUINEA   1922

The first appointment of a staff anthropologist to assist the administrator of the Australian New Guinea Territories led to expanded use of anthropologists in various functional areas by the Australians. Anthropologists did general ethnography as well as administratively defined problems.

Williams, F. E.
1939   Creed of a Government Anthropologist. Report of the Australian and New Guinea Association for the Advancement of Science, Vol. 24.

1951   The Blending of Cultures: An Essay on the Aims of Native Education. Port Moresby, Territory of Papua: Government Printer.

49 NEW GUINEA   1923

Section II of the Pan-Pacific Science Congress, Melbourne, passed a resolution asking the Commonwealth Government to support a faculty position in anthropology at the University of Sydney and to appoint an official anthropologist for the mandated territory of New Guinea.

Chinnery, W. P.
1933   Applied Anthropology in New Guinea. Report of the 21st Meeting of the Australian and New Zealand Association for the Advancement of Science. pp. 163-175.

Hogbin, H. Ian
1949   Government Chiefs in New Guinea. In Social Structure; Studies Presented to A. R. Radcliffe-Brown. London: Oxford University Press.

50-53 ANTHROPOLOGY IN USE

50   UNION OF SOUTH AFRICA   1925

        The government created an Ethnological section of the Native Affairs Department. Kuper notes, "the work of this body--later much expanded--has never gone much beyond the routine of making ethnological censuses, advising on the claims of various candidates for chiefships, and, more recently, divising pseudo-traditional forms of tribal administration" (Kuper 1973:128).

        Kuper, Adam
        1973   Anthropologists and Anthropology, the British School, 1922-1972. London: Allen Lane.

51   NEW GUINEA   1925

        A training scheme was organized for administrative personnel at the University of Sydney. It included special courses in anthropology.

        Mair, Lucy P.
        1948   Australia in New Guinea. London: Christophers.

52   UNITED STATES   1926

        The Catholic Anthropological Conference was organized at an informal meeting held at the Catholic University of America, Washington, D.C. The chief aims of the Conference were the advancement of anthropological science through the promotion of research and publication by missionaries and professional anthropologists as well as anthropological training among candidates for missionary work. The Conference published the journal entitled, Primitive Man, which later became Anthropological Quarterly.

        Luzbetak, Louis J.
        1961   Toward an Applied Missionary Anthropology. Anthropological Quarterly. 34:165-176.

        Miller, Elmer S.
        1970   The Christian Missionary, Agent of Secularization. Anthropological Quarterly. 43:14-22.

53   UNITED STATES   1926

        Manuel Gamio, who later came to be involved in the Instituto Indigenista Interamericano, was commissioned by the Social Science Research Council to do an analysis of Mexican immigration to the United States. The Mexican government briefly participated in sponsoring the project.

        Gamio, Manuel
        1971a   Mexican Immigration to the United States, a Study of Human Migration and Adjustment. New York: Dover.

BIBLIOGRAPHIC CHRONOLOGY 54–56

    1971b   The Life Story of the Mexican Immigrant, Autobiographic Documents. New York: Dover.

54   AFRICA   1926

The establishment of the International Institute of African Languages and Cultures was based on the need for scientific data relevant to problems of administrating colonial Africa. The institute was supported by the governments of Germany, France, United Kingdom, Belgium, Italy, and South Africa. The Institute emphasized research in problem areas, and published the journal entitled Africa.

International Institute of African Languages and Cultures
1937   Annual Report: the Work of the Institute in 1936. Africa. 10:108-9.

Lugard, F. D.
1928   The International Institute of African Languages and Cultures. Africa. 1:1-14.

Malinowski, Bronislaw
1929   Practical Anthropology. Africa. 2:23-38.

Richards, A. I.
1944   Practical Anthropology in the Lifetime of the International African Institute. Africa. 14:289-301.

55   NIGERIA   1927

C. W. Meek and P. Talbot were posted to Southern Nigeria in order to investigate the breakdown of local administration there. According to Kuper the role of government anthropologists did not become institutionalized in West Africa.

Kuper, Adam
1973   Anthropologists and Anthropology, the British School, 1922-1972. London: Allen Lane.

Meek, C. W.
1937   Law and Authority in a Nigerian Tribe. London: Oxford University Press.

56   TANGANYIKA   1928

District officer-anthropologist teams were developed on an experimental basis to improve administration. The anthropologist served as a staff consultant, providing information but not plans for action. The project carried out by G. Gordon Brown and A. M. Hutt was directed at improving administration among the Hehe. The primary goal was the administration of governance.

57–60 ANTHROPOLOGY IN USE

Brown, G. Gordon and A. M. Hutt
1935   Anthropology in Action. London: Oxford University Press.

57   UNITED STATES   1928

Franz Boas was one of the founding members of the Conference on Racial Differences sponsored by the National Research Council and the Social Science Research Council.

Stocking, George W., Jr.
1979   Anthropology as Kulturkampf: Science and Politics in the Career of Franz Boas. In The Uses of Anthropology. Walter Goldschmidt (ed.). (A special publication of the American Anthropological Association, Number 11.) Washington, D.C.: American Anthropological Association.

58   NIGERIA   1929

An investigating commission, in response to what were called the Aba riots in Southeastern Nigeria, recommended that administrative officers be assigned the duty of doing ethnographic research. By 1934, over 200 ethnographic reports were prepared.

Perham, Margery
1947   Native Administration in Nigeria. London: Oxford University Press.

59   EAST AFRICA   1930

The memorandum issued on native policy in East Africa gave official recognition of the importance of anthropology in the training of government administrators.

Smith, Edwin
1934   Anthropology and the Practical Man. Journal of the Royal Anthropological Institute. 64:xiii-xxxvii.

60   GREAT BRITAIN   1930

The phrase, "Applied Anthropology," according to H. Ian Hogbin, was first used by Radcliffe-Brown in a 1930 article.

Hogbin, H. Ian
1957   Anthropology as Public Service and Malinowski's Contribution to It. In Man and Culture, an Evaluation of the Work of Bronislaw Malinowski. R. Firth (ed.). London: Routledge and Kegan Paul.

Radcliffe-Brown, A. R.
1930   Applied Anthropology. Proceedings of the Australian and New Zealand Association for the Advancement of Science. pp. 267-80.

BIBLIOGRAPHIC CHRONOLOGY **61–65**

61 UNITED STATES   1932

   John Collier was appointed Commissioner of Indian Affairs in the
   Roosevelt administration.

   Spicer, Edward H.
   1977   Early Applications of Anthropology in North America.
           In Perspectives on Anthropology, 1976. Anthony F. C.
           Wallace et. al. (eds.). Washington, D.C.: American
           Anthropological Association. (A special publication of
           the American Anthropological Association, Number 10.)

62 NETHERLANDS INDIES   1933

   A survey of educational systems of Netherlands Indies assessed
   conditions and indicated aims of the native education program.

   Embree, Edwin R., Margaret Sargent Simon and W. Bryant Mumford
   1934   Island India Goes to School. Chicago: University of
           Chicago Press.

63 BECHUANALAND   1933

   Anthropologist Isaac Schapera was hired to document native law
   and customs as a guide to the administration.

   Schapera, Isaac
   1939   Anthropology and the Native Problem. South African
           Journal of Science. 36:89-103.

64 NETHERLANDS   1933

   Van Vollenhoven's classic compilation of Indonesian customary law,
   adat, was published. The Dutch administration was highly committed
   to the use of indirect rule, hence they used adat as the basis of
   civil law in these territories. Van Vollenhoven's studies were
   of significant practical benefit.

   Van Vollenhoven, C.
   1933   La Decouverte du Droit Indonesien. Paris.

65 UNITED STATES   1933

   The Civil Works Administration was inaugurated as a federal relief
   program to reduce unemployment. Money was allocated for hiring
   over fifteen hundred archaeological field laborers under the direction of the Smithsonian Institution. Extensive excavations were
   conducted, particularly in the Southeastern United States. A
   lull in activity followed the demise of the C.W.A. in 1934, but
   the creation of the Works Progress Administration in 1936 brought
   a resurgence of large-scale fieldwork which was to continue until
   World War II. This first period of massive government funding for
   archaeology not only resulted in an extensive amount of fieldwork,

but also served as a training device and professionalization experience for the next generation of American archaeologists.

Fitting, James E.
1973   The Development of North American Archaeology. Garden City, N.J.: Anchor Books.

66   UNITED STATES   1934

George Gordon Brown was appointed Principal of the Feleti School in American Samoa.

Carpenter, Edmund
1957   Obituary of George Brown. Human Organization. 16:14.

67   UNITED STATES   1935

Felix Keesing investigated aspects of Hawaiian homesteading patterns for the Hawaiian Legislature.

Kessing, Felix M.
1947   Applied Anthropology in Polynesia. Applied Anthropology. 6:(2):22-25.

68   UNITED STATES   1935

The organization of the Rio Grande Socio-economic Survey by the United States Department of Agriculture was completed. Directed at Native American, Mexican-American and Anglo-American residents of the Southwest, research focused on the cultural factors which had influenced land use. The concept of land use community was identified. This work was done under the aegis of the Soil Conservation Service established under the New Deal.

Kimball, Solon T. and John H. Provinse
1942   Navaho Social Organization in Land Use Planning. Applied Anthropology. 1:(4):18-250.

Provinse, John H.
1942   Cultural Factors in Land Use Planning. In The Changing Indian. Oliver La Farge (ed.). Norman: University of Oklahoma Press.

69   UNITED STATES   1935

The Historic Sites Act of 1935 (P.L. 74-292) was passed, declaring as national policy the preservation for public use of historic sites, buildings and objects. It led to the establishment of the Historic Sites Survey, the Historic American Building Survey, and the Historic American Engineering Record. The National Historic Landmarks program and its advisory board were established under the act to designate properties of historic value. The National Historic Landmarks program was the beginning of the National Register of Historic

Places which would later be expanded and strengthened by the National Historic Preservation Act of 1966 (P.L. 89-665) and by Executive Order 11593. These programs demonstrate increasing government interest in cultural resource management and the cataloging and assessment of historically significant properties.

Boisvert, Richard and Alvin Luckenbach (eds.)
1976   Kentucky's Heritage: A Public Concern. Lexington, Ky.: University of Kentucky, Department of Anthropology.

70   UNITED STATES   1936

The Applied Anthropology Unit was created to review prospects of certain American Indian Tribes to develop self-governance organizations in response to the Indian Reorganization Act of 1934. Research topics included settlement patterns, education policy, and prospects for economic development. The group's research had very little impact on the direction of political development. H. Scudder Mekeel was hired by John Collier as the first director. Participants included Julian Steward, Morris Opler, Claude Schaeffer, Abraham Halpern, Charles Wisdom, Margaret Welpley Fisher, David Rodnick and Gordon MacGregor.

Collier, John
1936   Instruction to Field Workers, Applied Anthropology Unit. Office of Indian Affairs, Applied Anthropology Unit.

1944   Collier Replies to Mekeel. American Anthropologist. 46:(3):424-25.

MacGregor, Gordon
1936   Washo Indians of the Sacramento Jurisdiction. Office of Indian Affairs, Applied Anthropology Unit.

n.d.   Report on the Pit River Indians of California. Office of Indian Affairs, Applied Anthropology Unit.

McNickle, D'Arcy
1979   Anthropology and the Indian Reorganization Act. In The Uses of Anthropology. Walter Goldschmidt (ed.). (A special publication of the American Anthropological Association, Number 11.) Washington, D.C.: American Anthropological Association.

Mekeel, H. Scudder
1936   Social Science and Reservation Programs. Indians at Work. IV:7.

1944   An Appraisal of the Indian Reorganization Act. American Anthropologist. 46:2.

Opler, Morris E.
1936   Report on Observations at Mescalero Reservation. Office of Indian Affairs, Applied Anthropology Unit.

Rodnick, David
1936   Report on the Indians of Kansas. Applied Anthropology Unit Report Series. Washington, D.C.: Office of Indian Affairs, Department of the Interior.

Schaeffer, C. E.
1936   Future Possibilities of Self-Government Among the Flathead. Office of Indian Affairs, Applied Anthropology Unit

Stirling, Gene
1936   Report on the Seminole Indians of Florida. Office of Indian Affairs, Applied Anthropology Unit.

Thompson, Laura
1956   U.S. Indian Reorganization Viewed as an Experiment in Social Action Research. Estudios Antropologicos Publicado en Homenaje a Doctor Manuel Gamio. Mexico: Direccion General de Publicaciones.

Wisdom, Charles
1936   Report on the Great Lake Chippewa. Office of Indian Affairs, Applied Anthropology Unit.

n.d.   Origin of Keetoowah Society. Office of Indian Affairs, Applied Anthropology Unit.

n.d.   Memorandum on the Present Condition of the Oklahoma Choctaw. Office of Indian Affairs, Applied Anthropology Unit.

71   UNITED STATES   1936

According to George Foster, Esther Lucille Brown was the first anthropologist to make significant contributions to anthropology and nursing. She also contributed to the development of the Russell Sage Foundation.

Brown, Esther Lucille
1936   Nursing as a Profession. New York: Russell Sage.

1948   Nursing for the Future. New York: Russell Sage.

1961   Newer Dimensions of Patient Care, Part 1, The Use of the Physical and Social Environment of the General Hospital for Therapeutic Purposes. New York: Russell Sage Foundation.

BIBLIOGRAPHIC CHRONOLOGY 72-74

1962 Newer Dimensions in Patient Care, Part 2, Improving Staff Motivation and Competence in the General Hospital. New York: Russell Sage.

1964 Newer Dimensions in Patient Care, Part 3, Patients as People. New York: Russell Sage.

72 UNITED STATES 1937

Ruth Underhill was employed by the so-called TC-BIA research group to study various aspects of Papago life. One facet which was selected for study was Papago place names. In early 1938 the TC-BIA submitted a report to the Office of Indian Affairs on place names. The report stimulated controversy because it was based on a minimal amount of field study. Papago Agency staff did the whole project over again with a greater emphasis on the Papago's viewpoint.

Papago Agency
n.d. Place Names on the Sells, Gila Bend and San Xavier Indian Reservations. Sells: Papago Agency, Department of the Interior.

73 NORTHERN RHODESIA 1937

F. Spearpoint was compound manager for the Roan Antelope Copper Mine. He was involved in developing the system by which native laborers were recruited and provided for between 1929 and 1937. Over the years the system was modified to fit better with the native ways of life and reportedly grew "more efficient." Spearpoint analyzed the contrast between European and African attitudes toward work, some dynamics of the kin-based social system, indigenous legal systems and the effects of European contact on natives. Although Spearpoint is not an anthropologist, he is a good observer and made use of cultural data.

Spearpoint, F.
1937 The African Native and the Rhodesian Copper Mines. Royal African Society Journal. 36:1-56.

74 UNITED STATES 1937

The Penncraft Resettlement Project, sponsored by the American Friends Service Committee, used an anthropologist as a consultant to create an independent community. Among other innovations the project made use of "mutual self-help" housing techniques.

Richardson, F. L. W., Jr.
1941 Community Resettlement in a Depressed Coal Region. Applied Anthropology. 1:(1):24-53.

75-77 ANTHROPOLOGY IN USE

    1942   Community Resettlement in a Depressed Coal Region II, Economic Problems of the New Community. Applied Anthropology. 3:(3):32-61.

Richardson, F. L. W., Jr. and R. C. Sheldon
1948   Community Resettlement in a Depressed Coal Region III, The Problem of Community Change: From Company Town to Planned Resettlement. Human Organization. 7:(4):1-27.

75 GREAT BRITAIN 1937

The Rhodes-Livingstone Institute, established by Sir Hubert Young, governor of Northern Rhodesia, focused on Central African studies. The Institute was to improve "native" and "non-native" relations and to determine the effect of culture contact on native African Society. The Institute was established independently of the government and directed by a board of trustees to investigate policy relevant issues. Early directors of the operation included Godfrey Wilson and Max Gluckman. About one-half of the Institute's budget was government supplied. The Institute is, "intended as a contribution to the scientific efforts now being made in various quarters to examine the effects upon native African Society of the impact of European civilization, by the formation in Africa itself of a center where the problem of establishing permanent and satisfactory relations between natives and non-natives...may form the subject of special study."

International Institute on African Languages and Cultures
1946   Notes and News. Africa. 16(2).

Mair, Lucy
1960   The Social Sciences in Africa, South of the Sahara: The British Contribution. Human Organization. 19:(3):98-107.

Wilson, Godfrey
1940   Anthropology as a Public Service. Africa. 13:43-60.

76 UNITED STATES 1937

The United States Department of Agriculture established the Technical Cooperation-Bureau of Indian Affairs Unit. TC-BIA was supported by the Soil Conservation Service but assisted the Bureau of Indian Affairs as a research unit. Various researches were carried out which focused on improving natural resource use.

Kennard, Edward A. and Gordon MacGregor
1953   Applied Anthropology in Government: United States. In Anthropology Today. A. L. Kroeber (ed.). Chicago: University of Chicago Press.

77 SUDAN 1938

S. F. Nadel was appointed Government Anthropologist in the Sudan.

BIBLIOGRAPHIC CHRONOLOGY 78–80

There he carried out work among the Nuba Tribes which resulted in the publication of The Nuba.

Nadel, S. F.
1947   The Nuba. London: Oxford University Press.

78   THE AMERICAS   1938

The Inter-American Indian Institute was established in Mexico with Manuel Gamio as its first director. The organization has encouraged direct action as well as more traditional anthropological activities.

Gamio, Manuel
1945   Some Considerations of Indianist Policy. In The Science of Man in the World Crisis. R. Linton (ed.). New York: Columbia University Press.

Instituto Indigenista Interamericano
1941   Instituto Indigenista Interamericano. America Indigena. 1:(1):1.

79   UNITED STATES   1938

The Sherman and Phoenix School Surveys in Indian education attempted to learn whether vocational training helped in post-school attendance adjustment.

MacGregor, Gordon and Armin Sterner
1939   The Pine Ridge Vocational Survey. Indian Education, 31, (November 1, 1939).

1940   The Sherman-California Survey. Indian Education, 41, (April 13, 1940).

80   UNITED STATES   1939

United States Department of Agriculture's Rural Life Studies, a series of six community studies in selected parts of the United States, were commissioned. They focused on community responses and potentials for change and tended toward holism. The team included anthropologists. Additional studies were planned but Congressional opposition developed.

Bell, Earl H.
1942   Culture of a Contemporary Rural Community, Sublette, Kansas. U.S. Department of Agriculture, Rural Life Studies, No. 2.

Kollmorgen, W. M.
1942   Culture of a Contemporary Rural Community, The Old Order Amish of Lancaster County, Pennsylvania. U.S. Department of Agriculture, Rural Life Studies, No. 4.

Leonard, Olen and Charles P. Loomis
1941   Culture of a Contemporary Rural Community, El Cerrito, New Mexico. U.S. Department of Agriculture, Rural Life Studies, No. 1.

Loomis, Charles P. and Nellie H. Loomis
1942   Skilled Spanish-American War-Industry Workers from New Mexico. Applied Anthropology. 2(1):33-36.

MacLiesh, Kenneth and Kimball Young
1942   Culture of a Contemporary Rural Community, Landoff, New Hampshire. U.S. Department of Agriculture, Rural Life Studies, No. 3.

Moe, E. O. and Carl C. Taylor
1942   Culture of a Contemporary Rural Community, Irwin, Iowa. U.S. Department of Agriculture, Rural Life Series, No. 5.

Olson, Philip
1964   Rural American Community Studies: The Survival of Public Ideology. Human Organization. 23(4):342-350.

Taylor, Carl C.
1945   Techniques of Community Study and Analysis as Applied to Modern Civilized Societies. In The Science of Man in the World Crisis. Ralph Linton (ed.). New York: Columbia University Press.

Wynne, Waller
1943   Culture of a Contemporary Rural Community, Harmony, Georgia. U.S. Department of Agriculture, Rural Life Studies, No. 6.

81   UNITED STATES   1939

Management and the Worker: An Account of a Research Program Conducted by the Western Electric Company, by Roethlisberger and Dickson was published. This study involved W. Lloyd Warner and was marked by an increase in the use of analysis techniques to identify the "informal" social system of the plant. Work in industrial research was encouraged through the formation of the Committee on Human Relations in Industry at the University of Chicago. Warner served as its first chairman. Another anthropologically trained associate of the committee was Burleigh B. Gardner. Gardner, known for his research in the urban south, ultimately became director of personnel research for Western Electric. Gardner's association with the committee ended and he was replaced by William F. Whyte. This group benefitted methodologically from the efforts of Eliott D. Chapple.

Buchsbaum, Herbert J., Samuel Laderman, Sidney Garfield, Andrew H. Whitefore, William F. Whyte and Burleigh B. Gardner
1946   From Conflict to Cooperation: A Study in Union-Management Relations. Applied Anthropology. 5(4).

Chapple, E. D.
1941   Organizational Problems in Industry. Applied Anthropology.
            1(1):2-9.

1949   The Interaction Chronograph: Its Evolution and Present
            Application. Personnel. XXV(4):295-307.

1953   Applied Anthropology in Industry. In Anthropology Today.
            A. L. Kroeber (ed.). Chicago: University of Chicago Press.

Chapple, E. D. and E. F. Wright
1946   How to Supervise People in Industry. Chicago and New
            York: National Foreman's Institute.

Gardfield, Sidney and William F. Whyte
1951   The Collective Bargaining Process: A Human Relations
            Analysis. Human Organization. 10(1):28-32.

Gardner, Burleigh B. and William F. Whyte
            The Man in the Middle: Position and Problems of the
            Foreman. Applied Anthropology. 4(2).

Horsfall, Alexander and Conrad M. Arensberg
1949   Teamwork and Productivity in a Shoe Factory. Human
            Organization. 8(1):13-25.

Roethlisberger, F. J. and W. J. Dickson
1939   Management and the Worker: An Account of a Research
            Program Conducted by the Western Electric Company,
            Hawthorne Works, Chicago. Cambridge: Harvard University
            Press.

Warner, W. Lloyd and J. O. Low
1947   The Social System of the Modern Factory. New Haven:
            Yale University Press.

Whyte, William F.
1948   Incentives for Productivity: The Bundy Tubing Company
            Case. Applied Anthropology. 7(2):1-16.

1951   Pattern for Industrial Peace. New York: Harper and
            Brothers.

UNITED STATES   1939

Under secretary of agriculture, M. L. Wilson and rural sociologist Carl Taylor organized a conference in Washington D.C. which was to lead to increasing the contribution of disciplines other than rural sociology to the Bureau of Agricultural Economics within the U.S. Department of Agriculture. Anthropologists participating in the conference included Conrad Arensberg, Horace Miner, John Provinse, Robert Redfield and William Lloyd Warner.

83-86 ANTHROPOLOGY IN USE

Spicer, Edward H.
1977   Early Applications of Anthropology in North America. In
            Perspectives on Anthropology, 1976. Anthony F. C. Wallace
            et. al. (eds.). Washington, D.C.: American Anthropological
            Association. (A special publication of the American
            Anthropological Association, Number 10.)

83   UNITED STATES   1939

The Committee for National Morale was established to, "consider the
ways in which anthropology and psychology could be applied to the
improvement of national morale during wartime" (Partridge and Eddy
1978:28). The committee consisted of Gregory Bateson, Eliott
Chapple, Lawrence K. Frank and Margaret Mead.

Bateson, Gregory and Margaret Mead
1941   Principles of Morale Building. Journal of Educational
            Sociology. 15:206-220.

84   MEXICO   1939

Maurice Swadesh became the director of a national program for the
introduction of alphabets and written materials in various languages.
Swadesh took specific responsibility for the Tarascan program.
Primers and other instructional materials were developed.

Spicer, Edward H.
1977   Early Applications of Anthropology in North America. In
            Perspectives on Anthropology, 1976. Anthony F. C. Wallace
            et. al. (eds.). Washington, D.C.: American Anthropological
            Association. (A special publication of the American
            Anthropological Association, Number 10.)

Swadesh, Mauricio
1940   La Nueva Filologia, Coleccion "Siglo xx," Biblioteca del
            Maestro, Mexico: D. F.

85   SUDAN   1940

E. E. Evans-Pritchard served as Bimbashi (Lieutenant Colonel) in
the Sudanese Defense Force.

Evans-Pritchard, E. E.
1974   A Bibliography of the Writings of E. E. Evans-Pritchard.
            London: Tavistock.

86   GREAT BRITAIN   1940

Margaret Read was appointed head of the Colonial Department of the
University of London, Institute of Education. The department
offered training, which included anthropology, to colonial administrators.

Read, Margaret
1943   Notes on the Work of the Colonial Department, University of London Institute of Education. Applied Anthropology. 3(1):8-9.

1950   Educational Problems in Non-Autonomous Territories. Principles and Methods of Colonial Administration. C. M. MacInnes (ed.). London: Butterworths Scientific Publications.

UNITED STATES   1940

The Committee on Food Habits was created by the National Research Council to obtain scientific data on American nutritional levels and to ascertain how American nutritional levels could be improved. The plan of action of the committee included general guidelines for action. The anthropologists associated with the committee included Ruth Benedict, Rhoda Metraux, Allison Davis, and Carl Guthe. Margaret Mead served the committee as Executive Secretary.

Bennett, John W., Harvey L. Smith and Herbert Passin
1942   Food and Culture in Southern Illinois, A Preliminary Report. American Sociological Review. 7:645-660.

1943a   Dietary Patterns and Food Habits. Journal of the American Dietetics Association. 19:1-5.

1943b   The Problem of Changing Food Habits: with Suggestions for Psychoanalytic Contributions. Bulletin of the Menninger Clinic. 7:57-61.

1943c   The Problem of Changing Food Habits. In The Problem of Changing Food Habits. Washington, D.C.: National Research Council.

Metraux, Rhoda
1943   Qualitative Attitude Analysis, A Technique for the Study of Verbal Behavior. In The Problem of Changing Food Habits. Washington, D.C.: National Research Council.

Montgomery, Edward and John W. Bennett
1979   Anthropological Studies of Food and Nutrition: The 1940s and the 1970s. In The Uses of Anthropology. Walter Goldschmidt (ed.). (A special publication of the American Anthropological Association, Number 11.) Washington, D.C.: American Anthropological Association.

National Research Council, Committee on Food Habits
1943   The Problem of Changing Food Habits. Washington, D.C.: National Research Council.

1945   Manual for the Study of Food Habits. Washington, D.C.: National Research Council.

88-90 ANTHROPOLOGY IN USE

Passin, Herbert and John W. Bennett
1943 Social Process and Dietary Change. In The Problems of Changing Food Habits. Washington, D. C.: National Research Council.

Powdermaker, Hortense
1943 Summary of Methods of a Field Work Class Cooperating with the Committee on Food Habits. In The Problem of Changing Food Habits. Washington, D.C.: National Research Council.

88   MEXICO   1940

As part of the research program of the Department of Native Affairs a number of general studies of Indian communities with emphasis on mestizo-Indian relations. Spicer suggests that one of the "most successful" of these studies was carried out by A. Fabila in Yaqui communities in northwest Mexico. Based on this research a new form of landholding was recommended.

Fabila, Alfonso
1940 Las Tribus Yaquis Y su Anhelada Auto-Determination. Mexico: Departmento de Asuntos Indigenas.

89   GREAT BRITAIN   1940

Parliament passed the Colonial Development and Welfare Act which provided for among other things for colonial research. This occurred because of Lord Hailey's Africa Survey. By the 1950s over 1,000,000 pounds had been spent. Only a small portion of this was allocated to anthropology. Following the war these funds were allocated by the Colonial Social Science Research Council which included Raymond Firth and Audrey Richards.

Hailey, W. M.
1938 An African Survey. London.

Kuper, Adam
1973 Anthropologists and Anthropology, the British School 1922-1972. London: Allen Lane.

90   UNITED STATES   1941

The American Anthropological Association passed a resolution which encouraged the participation of their members in the war effort. "Be it resolved: that the American Anthropological Association place itself and its resources and the specialized skills and knowledge of its members at the disposal of the country for the successful prosecution of the war."

American Anthropological Association
1942 Resolution. American Anthropologist. 44:289.

BIBLIOGRAPHIC CHRONOLOGY 91–94

Beals, Ralph L.
1969   Politics of Social Research, an Inquiry into the Ethics and Responsibilities of Social Scientists. Chicago: Aldine Publishing.

91 UNITED STATES   1941

Rosalie H. Wax worked as a researcher in the University of California's Evacuation and Resettlement Study and worked as an anthropologist in both the Gila River and Tule Lake Relocation Centers of the War Relocation Agency.

Thomas, D. S. and R. S. Nishomoto
1946   The Spoilage. Berkeley: University of California Press.

Wax, Rosalie H.
1953   The Destruction of a Democratic Impulse. Human Organization. 11(1):34-37.

92 UNITED STATES   1941

Anthropologist Kalervo Oberg was employed as Associate Coordinator of the Middle Rio Grande Board of the Soil Conservation Service of the United States Department of Agriculture. This organization served to coordinate various Federal Conservation and Development programs in that area of the Southwest.

Oberg, Kalervo, Allan G. Harper and Andrew R. Cordova
1943   Man and Resources in the Middle Rio Grande Valley. Albuquerque: University of New Mexico Press.

93 UNITED STATES   1941

The Society for Applied Anthropology was established. The Society has provided for an expressive outlet for the work of applied anthropologists in its journal and annual meetings. In its early days the Society served as an intermediary between its members and potential clients. The Society has also served to define ethnical standards.

Foster, George M.
1969   Applied Anthropology. Little, Brown and Company, Boston.

94 UNITED STATES   1941

The Indian Personality and Administration Research Project was organized by the Bureau of Indian Affairs to evaluate the impact of its administrative policies on Native American Populations and to identify effects on personality. The project made early use of action research techniques. It produced a number of interesting publications, but had little effect on policy.

Collier, John
1945   The United States Indian Administration as a Laboratory of Ethnic Relations. Social Research. 12:265-303.

Joseph, Alice, Rosamond B. Spicer and Jane Chesky
1949   The Desert People: A Study of the Papago Indians. Chicago: University of Chicago Press.

Kelly, William H.
1954   Applied Anthropology in the Southwest. American Anthropologist. 56:709-719.

Kluckhohn, Clyde and Dorothea C. Leighton
1946   The Navaho. Cambridge: Harvard University Press.

Leighton, Dorothea C. and John Adair
1946   People of the Middle Place: A Study of the Zuni Indians. New Haven: Human Relations Area Files.

Leighton, Dorothea C. and Clyde Kluckhohn
1947   Children of the People. Cambridge: Harvard University Press.

MacGregor, Gordon
1946   Warriors Without Weapons. Chicago: University of Chicago Press.

Thompson, Laura
1950   Action Research Among American Indians. Scientific Monthly. LXX:34-40.

1951   Personality and Government. Ediciones del Instituto Indigenista Interamericano. Mexico: D.F.

1970   Exploring American Indian Communities in Depth. In Women in the Field, Anthropological Experiences. Peggy Golde (ed.). Chicago: Aldine.

Thompson, Laura and Alice Joseph
1944   The Hopi Way. New York: Russell Sage.

95   UNITED STATES   1941

The War Relocation Authority was created to administer the camps established for the Japanese-Americans interned by military authorities during the Second World War. A social science research program was established at the one camp which was under the administrative control of the Bureau of Indian Affairs and Commissioner John Collier. After substantial administrative difficulty at various camps social science research programs were established at other locations. The researcher role termed "community analyst" was filled by anthropologists and sociologists.

Arensberg, Conrad M.
1942   Report on a Developing Community, Poston, Arizona.
            Applied Anthropology. 2(1):2-21.

Brown, G. Gordon
1945   War Relocation Authority, Gila River Project, Rivers,
            Arizona, Community Analysis Section, May 12 to July 7,
            1945, Final Report. Applied Anthropology. 4(4):1-49.

Embree, John F.
1943   Resistance to Freedom--An Administrative Problem.
            Applied Anthropology. 2(4):10-14.

1943   The Relocation of Persons of Japanese Ancestry in the
            United States: Some Causes and Effects. Journal of
            the Washington Academy of Sciences. 33(8).

1943   Dealing with Japanese-Americans. Applied Anthropology.
            2(2):37-43.

1944   Community Analysis--An Example of Anthropology in Government.
            American Anthropologist. 46(3).

Hansen, Asael T.
1946   Community Analysis at Heart Mountain Relocation Center.
            Applied Anthropology. 5(3):15-25.

Kimball, Solon T.
1946   Community Government in the War Relocation Centers.
            Washington, D.C.: Government Printing Office.

Leighton, Alexander H. et. al.
1943   Assessing Public Opinion in a Dislocated Community.
            Public Opinion Quarterly. 7(4).

1945   The Governing of Men: General Principles and Recommendations
            Based on Experience at a Japanese Relocation Camp.
            Princeton, N.J.: Princeton University Press.

Loumala, Katharine
1946   California Takes Back its Japanese Evacuees, The Readjust-
            ment of California to the Return of the Japanese Evacuees.
            Applied Anthropology. 5(3):25-39.

1947   Community Analysis by the War Relocation Authority Outside
            the Relocation Centers. Applied Anthropology. 6(1):25-31.

1948   Research and the Records of the War Relocation Authority.
            Applied Anthropology. 7(1):23-32.

Opler, Marvin K.
1945   A Sumo Tournament at Tule Lake Center. American Anthropo-
            logist. 47:134-39.

Provinse, John H. and Solon T. Kimball
1946   Building New Communities During Wartime. American Sociological Review. 11:396-410.

Spicer, Edward H.
1946a   The Use of Social Scientists by the War Relocation Authority. Applied Anthropology. 5(2):16-36.

1946b   Impounded People: Japanese-Americans in the Relocation Centers. Department of the Interior, War Relocation Authority, Washington, D.C.

1952a   Reluctant Cotton-Pickers: Incentive to Work in a Japanese Relocation Center. In Human Problems in Technological Change. Edward H. Spicer (ed.). New York: Russell Sage Foundation.

1952b   Resistance to Freedom: Resettlement from the Japanese Relocation Centers During World War II. In Human Problems in Technological Change. New York: Russell Sage Foundation.

1979   Anthropologists and the War Relocation Authority. In The Uses of Anthropology. Walter Goldschmidt (ed.). (A special publication of the American Anthropological Association, Number 11.) Washington, D.C.: American Anthropological Association.

War Relocation Authority
1947   WRA--A Story of Human Conservation. Washington, D.C.: U.S. Department of the Interior.

96   UNITED STATES   1941

Initial issue of the journal Applied Anthropology, later to be called Human Organization, was published.

Society for Applied Anthropology
1941   Editorial Statement. Applied Anthropology. 1(1):1-2.

Srb, Jozetta H.
1966   Human Organization: The Growth and Development of a Professional Journal. Human Organization. 25(3):187-197.

97   UNITED STATES   1942

The Rosebud Sioux Employment Project, sponsored by the U.S. Office of Indian Affairs and the University of South Dakota, was to determine the nature of the Sioux's participation in the regional economy.

Useem, John, Gordon MacGregor and Ruth Hill Useem
1943   Wartime Employment and Cultural Adjustments of the Rosebud Sioux. Applied Anthropology. 2(2):1-9.

BIBLIOGRAPHIC CHRONOLOGY 98-101

98 SUDAN 1942

In the British Colonies a large number of administrative officers received training in anthropology. Some of these contributed useful works to the basic ethnographic literature on the administered peoples. One example is P. P. Howell who not only worked as a District Officer in Anglo-Egyptian Sudan but ultimately obtained a D. Phil. (oxon) in anthropology. A most interesting product of his work is A Manual of Nuer Law.

Howell, P. P.
1954   A Manual of Nuer Law, Being an Account of Customary Law, its Evolution and Development in the Courts Established by the Sudan Government. London: International African Institute by Oxford University Press.

99 UNITED STATES 1942

The Second World War stimulated studies of national character of both enemies and allies. Geoffrey Gorer was requested a few months after Pearl Harbor to submit a report on "Japanese Character Structure and Propaganda" to the Committee on Intercultural Relations. Gorer suggested a relationship between the Japanese patterns of toilet training and the brutal way they fought their wars.

Gorer, Geoffrey
1948   Themes in Japanese Culture. In Personal Character and Cultural Milieu. D. Haring (ed.). Edwards Bros.: Ann Arbor, Mich.

100 GREAT BRITAIN 1943

The Devonshire Training Scheme developed for British Colonial Service Officers included anthropology.

British Colonial Service
1946   Post-War Training for the Colonial Service, Report of the Committee appointed by the Secretary of State for the Colonies. London: H. M. Stationery Office.

101 UNITED STATES 1943

Far Eastern Civil Affairs Training School was established to provide personnel trained to deal with administering areas captured by the allies from the Japanese. The school, established at the University of Chicago, was directed by Fred Eggan. John Embree also participated. The program included culture change training.

Embree, John E.
1949   American Military Government. In Social Structure, Studies Presented to A. R. Radcliffe-Brown. M. Fortes (ed.). London: Oxford University Press.

102-105 ANTHROPOLOGY IN USE

102 NORTHERN RHODESIA 1943

As director of the Rhodes-Livingstone Institute, British Social Anthropologist Max Gluckman, developed a major applied anthropology research project which examined government policy as it related to the political organization of the Barotse.

Gluckman, Max
1943   Administrative Organization of the Barotse Native Authorities. Communication 1, Northern Rhodesia: Rhodes-Livingstone Institute.

1955   The Judicial Process Among the Barotse of Northern Rhodesia. Manchester: University of Manchester Press.

103 INDIA 1944

The anthropologist, Christoph von Furer-Haimendorf, became involved in a variety of social programs when appointed tribal advisor to the government of Hyderabad.

von Furer-Haimendorf, Christoph
1944   Aboriginal Education in Hyderabad. Indian Journal of Social Work. 5(2).

104 UNITED STATES 1944

Prior to the litigation stimulated by the Indian Claims Commission Act of 1946 there were many Indian tribes which filed suit against the American government for lost land. Stewart suggests that the number of anthropologists contributing to the preparation of these cases was quite limited. One such case which was assisted by an anthropologist was filed by the Indians of California. These people were aided by C. Hart Merriam, a biologist turned ethnologist. A decision was reached in this case in 1944.

Stewart, Omer C.
1961   Kroeber and the Indian Claims Commission Cases. Alfred L. Kroeber: A Memorial. Kroeber Anthropological Society Papers, No. 25 (Fall).

105 UNITED STATES 1944

The Navaho Door was published, it attempted to "educate and influence" the professional staff which provided health care to Navajo people. It argued against the displacement of traditional Navajo curing practices and had an impact on government policy. This represented an important attempt to bring the cultural relativism perspective to health planning.

Leighton, Alexander H. and Dorothea C. Leighton
1944   The Navaho Door. Cambridge: Harvard University Press.

Leighton, Dorothea C.
1972   Anthropology in the Medical Context. Medical Anthropology Newsletter. 4(1):1-3.

106 UNITED STATES   1944

The Foreign Morale Analysis Division was created as part of the Office of War Information. This organization provided social science analysis of various data sources concerning the Japanese and their morale. The organization provided service to the Departments of State, War, and Navy for various outposts in Asia and the Pacific. The project developed out of an early attempt to make studies of the Japanese as represented by the internees of the relocation camps. The project team included various types of social scientists. The anthropologists among them included Clyde Kluckhohn, Morris Opler, Ruth Benedict, John Embree, Frederick Hulse, Dorothea Leighton, Katherine Spencer, David Aberle, Alexander Leighton, and Iwao Ishino.

Benedict, Ruth
1946   The Chrysanthemum and the Sword. Boston: Houghton Mifflin.

Leighton, Alexander
1949   Human Relations in a Changing World, Observations on the Use of the Social Sciences. New York: Dutton.

107 OCEANIA   1944

"Civil Affairs Handbooks" were published by the Office of the Chief of Naval Operations. These handbooks included ethnological data for administrative staff in anticipation of the occupation of Japanese held Pacific Territories. This work was largely the responsibility of George P. Murdock. This resulted in monographs on the Marshalls, Marianas, the Carolines, and others.

Office of the Chief of Naval Operations
1944   Civil Affairs Handbook, West Caroline Islands, OPNAV 50E-7. Washington, D.C.: Office of the Chief of Naval Operations, Navy Department.

108 GREAT BRITAIN   1945

The Colonial Social Science Research Council (C.S.S.R.C.) was set up. The majority of C.S.S.R.C. fellowships were given to anthropologists working in Africa, thus allowing a dramatic expansion of the profession after World War II. The shortage of trained British people resulted in the awarding of some fellowships to Americans.

Kuper, Adam
1973   Anthropologists and Anthropology, the British School, 1922-1972. London: Allen Lane.

109–113 ANTHROPOLOGY IN USE

109   INDIA   1945

        W. H. Wiser, a frequent contributor to the social anthropological literature on rural India, started organizational work leading to the creation of India Village Service. I.V.S. was a privately funded experimental program which was to devise techniques for rural development in Uttar Pradesh. It was funded by various missionary groups. I.V.S. was committed to community development ideology.

        Wiser, W. H.
        1958   India Village Service, Retrospect and Prospect. Marehra, District Etah, Uttar Pradesh: India Village Service.

110   UNITED STATES   1945

        Human Relations in Industry, by Burleigh Gardner, was published. The book remained a widely used textbook in the industrial relations field for a decade. Gardner, who was trained in anthropology, had been associated with the personnel department of Western Electric.

        Gardner, Burleigh B. and David G. Moore
        1945   Human Relations in Industry. Chicago: Richard D. Irwin.

111   UNITED STATES   1945

        Lauriston Sharp served as Assistant Chief of the Division of Southeast Asian Affairs in the Department of State. Sharp's co-workers included Cora Dubois and Raymond Kennedy. Following this experience Sharp developed the program of instruction in applied anthropology at Cornell.

        Smith, Robert J.
        1974   Introduction. In Social Organization and the Applications of Anthropology, Essays in Honor of Lauriston Sharp. Ithaca: Cornell University Press.

112   AUSTRALIA   1945

        The inclusion of anthropological training for district and educational officers in Australian Papua and New Guinea. The training was necessary for promotion and included government, geography, land use, history, and tropical hygiene.

        Mair, Lucy P.
        1948   Australia in New Guinea. London: Christophers.

113   UNITED STATES   1945

        The School of Naval Administration at Stanford was established to prepare Naval personnel for work in Guam, American Samoa, as well as former Japanese Mandate territories. The associate director in charge of training was an anthropologist.

Kessing, Felix M.
1949   Experiments in Training Overseas Administrators. Human Organization. 8(4):20-22.

United States Navy Department
1948   Handbook on the Trust Territory of the Pacific Islands. Washington, D.C.: Office of the Chief of Naval Operations, Department of the Navy.

114   NORTHERN RHODESIA   1945

Working as an auxiliary to the Native Land Tenure Committee a group of researchers from the Rhodes-Livingstone Institute undertook a survey of the Plateau Tonga of Mazabuka District of Northern Rhodesia. The team included anthropologist Max Gluckman. This research was directed at providing information concerning "proposals to establish a system of controlled and improved land-usage among the Tonga." The government had expressed concern that a class of large land owners was developing which was going to inevitably displace the subsistence farmer. The submitted report suggested that these concerns were unfounded. The large land owners were shown to represent less than one percent of the population and that they derived their land through customary law. The report is specifically focused upon policy questions and makes explicite policy recommendations.

Allen, W., Max Gluckman, D. U. Peters, and C. G. Trapnell
1948   Land Holding and Land Use Among the Plateau Tonga of Mazabuka District. Rhodes-Livingston Papers No. 14. Rhodes-Livingstone Institute: Livingstone.

115   UNITED STATES   1945

Various anthropologists serve the American Occupation forces in the post-war period. Anthropologists came to be associated with the American Military Governments in Japan, the Pacific, and Germany. In these situations they served as researchers and consultants. This involvement resulted in a number of studies. Two of the most complex were Rodnick's study (1948) of civilian attitudes toward occupation and reconstruction in the Hesse region of Germany, and Leighton's study (1949) of aspects of the Japanese response to the war.

Bennett, John W.
1951   Community Research in the Japan Occupation. Clearing House Bulletin of Research. Human Organization. 1(3):1-2.

Gladwin, Thomas
1950   Civil Administration on Truk: A Rejoinder. Human Organization. 9(4):15-23.

Embree, John F.
1946   Military Government in Saipan and Tinian, a Report on the Organization of Susupe and Chuco, Together with Notes on the Attitudes of the People Involved. Applied Anthropology. 5(1):1-39.

Hall, Edward T.
1949   Military Government on Truk. Human Organization. 9(2):25-30.

Leighton, Alexander H.
1949   Human Relations in a Changing World: Observations on the Use of the Social Sciences. New York: E. P. Dutton.

Rodnick, David
1948   Postwar Germans, An Anthropologist's Account. New Haven: Yale University Press.

116   LIBYA   1945

S. F. Nadel served the British Military Administration as Secretary for Native Affairs.

Fortes, Meyer
1957   Siegfried Frederick Nadel, 1903-1956, a Memoir. In The Theory of Social Structure, S. F. Nadel. London: Cohen and West.

117   LIBYA   1945

E. E. Evans-Pritchard was appointed tribal affairs officer in Cyrenaica with the British military administration. Evans-Pritchard worked as a consultant and made policy recommendations.

Evans-Pritchard, E. E.
1949   The Sanusi of Cyrenaica. London: Oxford University Press.

James, Wendy
1973   The Anthropologist as Reluctant Imperialist. In Anthropology and the Colonial Encounter. Talal Asad (ed.). New York: Humanities Press.

118   UNITED STATES   1946

The hearings which were organized concerning the legislation which created the Indian Claims Commission had few participating anthropologists. These were A. V. Kidder and Gene Weltfish who testified for the American Civil Liberties Union.

Stewart, Omer C.
1961   Kroeber and the Indian Claims Commission Cases. Kroeber Anthropological Society Paper No. 25, Alfred L. Kroeber, a Memorium.

119   UNITED STATES   1946

The first volume of The Handbook of South American Indians was published. This encyclopedic work was, "initiated as a wartime activity under a State Department program for promoting cultural relations with Latin America" (Beals 1969:55).

Beals, Ralph L.
1969   Politics of Social Research, an Inquiry into the Ethics and Responsibilities of Social Scientists. Chicago: Aldine Publishing Company.

Steward, Julian H.
1946-59   Handbook of South American Indians, Vols. I-VII. Washington, D.C.: U.S. Government Printing Office.

120 AUSTRALIA   1946

School of Pacific Administration was established to give training, including anthropology, to administrators of Papua and New Guinea. The school is supported by the Commonwealth Department of Territories.

Elkin, A. P.
1953   Australia and New Zealand. In International Directory of Anthropological Institutions. William L. Thomas, Jr. and Anna M. Pikelis (eds.). New York: Wenner-Gren.

121 MICRONESIA   1946

The Micronesian comprehensive survey was carried out. The survey, sponsored by the United States Commercial Company, dealt with economics, anthropology, and administrative management. The social scientists focused on regional variations in the population's relationship with the sea and land.

Bascom, William R.
1947   Economic and Human Resources--Ponape. Eastern Carolines, U.S. Commercial Company.

Mason, Leonard E.
1947   Economic and Human Resources--Marshal Islands. U.S. Commercial Company.

Oliver, Douglas L. (ed.)
1951   Planning Micronesia's Future: A Summary of the United States Commercial Company's Economic Survey of Micronesia, 1946. Cambridge: Harvard University Press.

Pelzer, Karl and Edward T. Hall
1947   Economic and Human Resources--Truk Islands, Central Carolines. U.S. Commercial Company.

Useem, John
1947   Economic and Human Resources--Yap and Palau, Western Carolines. U.S. Commercial Company.

122 UNITED STATES   1946

The establishment of the Indian Claims Commission created many opportunities for ethnohistoric, archaeological, and ethnographic research for professional anthropologists. The commission, created in response to the Indian Claims Act of 1946, was to resolve issues associated with Indian land title, use, and occupancy. The act allowed most native groups in the United States to sue for compensation for lost lands.

Baerreis, David A.
1974   Anthropological Report on the Chippewa, Ottawa, and Potowatomi Indians in Northeastern Illinois and the Identity of the Mascoutens. New York: Garland.

Beals, Ralph L. and James A. Hester
1974   Indian Land Use and Occupancy in California. New York: Garland.

Bell, Robert E.
1974   Wichita Indian Archaeology and Ethnology: A Pilot Study. New York: Garland.

Chapman, Carl H.
1974   A Preliminary Survey of Missouri Archaeology. New York: Garland.

Dobyns, Henry F.
1974   Prehistoric Indian Occupation Within the Eastern Area of the Yuman Complex: A Study in Applied Archaeology. New York: Garland.

Dobyns, Henry F. and Robert C. Euler
1974   Socio-Political Structure and Ethnic Group Concept of the Pai. New York: Garland.

Ellis, Florence H.
1974   Anthropological Data Pertaining to the Taos Land Claim. New York: Garland.

Elmendorf, William W.
1974   Structure of Twana Culture. New York: Garland.

Grosscup, Gordon L.
1974   Northern Paiute Archaeology. New York: Garland.

Gussow, Zachary
1974   An Anthropological Report on the Sac, Fox and Iowa Indians. New York: Garland.

Hackenberg, Robert A.
1974   Papago Indians: Aboriginal Land Use and Occupancy. New York: Garland.

1974   Aboriginal Land Use and Occupancy of the Pima-Maricopa. New York: Garland.

Harvey, Herbert R.
1974   The Luiseno--Analysis of Change in Patterns of Land Tenure and Social Structure. New York: Garland.

Heizer, Robert F.
1974   Indians of California. New York: Garland.

Jablow, Joseph
1974   Illinois, Kickapoo and Potawatami Indians. New York: Garland.

Kroeber, A. L.
1974   Basic Report on California Indian Land Holdings. New York: Garland.

Lurie, Nancy Oestreich
1955   Anthropology and Indian Claims Litigation: Problems, Opportunities, and Recommendations. Ethnohistory. 2:357-375.

MacGregor, Gordon
1955   Anthropology in Government: United States. In Yearbook of Anthropology--1955. New York: Wenner-Gren.

Manners, Robert A.
1974   An Ethnographic Report on the Hualapai (Walapai) Indians of Arizona. New York: Garland.

Steward, Julian H.
1974   Aboriginal and Historical Groups of the Ute Indians of Utah; an Analysis with Supplement. New York: Garland.

Stout, David B., Erminie W. Voegelin and Emily J. Blasingham
1974   Indians of E. Missouri, W. Illinois, and S. Wisconsin, from the Proto-Historic Period to 1804. New York: Garland.

Taylor, Herbert C., Jr.
1974   Anthropological Investigation of the Tillamook Indians. New York: Garland.

Train, Percy
1974   Medicinal Uses of Plants by Indian Tribes of Nevada. New York: Garland.

United States Indian Claims Commission
1974   Commission Findings on the Sac, Fox and Iowa Indians. New York: Garland.

1974   Commission Findings on the Chippewa Indians. New York: Garland.

Voegelin, Erminie W. and E. J. Blasingham
1974   Anthropological Report on the Indian Occupancy of Royce Areas 77 and 78. New York: Garland.

123-126 ANTHROPOLOGY IN USE

Voget, Fred W.
1974   Osage Research Project. New York: Garland.

123   INDIA   1946

The Government of India, Department of Anthropology was established to do basic and applied research which included the development of culturally appropriate texts for village schools and a comprehensive study of the Andaman Islanders.

Majumdar, D. N.
1948   Department of Anthropology, Government of India. American Anthropologist. 50(3):578-81.

124   UNITED STATES   1946

Along with W. Lloyd Warner, Burleigh B. Gardner established Social Research, Inc. to engage in consultation work with businesses. The organization was staffed also by psychologists and sociologists. The company has done work in market research, business relations and social change. One of the earliest clients was Sears Roebuck and Company for which Social Research, Inc. developed an employee attitude survey scheme as part of a management information system.

Gardner, Burleigh B.
1978   Doing Business with Management. In Applied Anthropology in America. Elizabeth M. Eddy and William L. Partridge (eds.). New York: Columbia University Press.

125   NEW ZEALAND   1946

New Zealand Council for Educational Research sponsored research dealing with the influence of the city on a Maori community.

Beaglehole, E. and P. Beaglehole
1946   Some Modern Maoris. Wellington: New Zealand Council for Education Research.

126   MEXICO   1947

The Papaloapan Resettlement Project was made necessary by the construction of a large scale hydrological project of the Mexican government. Although the project would result in significant positive impact on food production, it would also result in the displacement of large numbers of Mazatec, Chinantec and Popoloca Indian villages. The resettlement program was the responsibility of Instituto Nacional Indigenista. The project strategy called for thorough base-line research, cooperative, non-coercive planning of the project by anthropologists and local leadership, and the maintenance of a significant number of pre-migration life ways.

Villa-Rojas, Alfonso
1955   Los Mazatecos y el Problema Indigena de la Cuenca del Papaloapan. Mexico D.F. Memorias del Instituto Nacional Indigenista, Vol. 7.

127   HAITI   1947

Marbial Valley Project was started to begin the process by which illiteracy, poverty and ill health in a rural Haiti Region could be conquered. The project started with survey research done by anthropologist Alfred Metraux. Based on these research activities, change programs were mounted. Later, other projects were carried out by other anthropologists. The project, a cooperative effort of UNESCO and the government of Haiti, was a very early example of the use of research working in conjunction with development activities.

Metraux, Alfred
1949   Anthropology and the UNESCO Pilot-Project of Marbial (Haiti). America Indigena. 9:183-194.

Sylvain, Jeanne G.
1949   La Infancia Campesina en el Valle del Marbial, Haiti. America Indigena. 9:299-332.

UNESCO
1951   The Haiti Pilot Project, Phase One. (Monograph on Fundamental Education No. 4.) UNESCO Publication No. 796.

128   MICRONESIA   1947

The Coordinated Investigation of Micronesian Anthropology (CIMA) project, funded by the United States Navy, was to provide comprehensive ethnographic data on the peoples of Micronesia. The project involved 35 anthropologists, including Spoehr, Murdock, Goodenough, Spiro, Lessa, and Barnett.

Barnett, H. G.
1956   Anthropology in Administration. Evanston: Row, Peterson.

Cooledge, Harold J.
1946   The Pacific Science Conference. Far Eastern Survey. 15:25 (December).

Lessa, William A.
1950   The Place of Ulithi in the Yap Empire. Human Organization. 9(1):16-18.

Pacific Science Board
1950   Fourth Annual Report, 1950. Washington, D.C.: Pacific Science Board, National Research Council.

Spoehr, A.
1954   Saipan, the Ethnology of a War Devastated Island. Fieldiana: Anthropology. Vol. XLI.

Useem, John
1947   Applied Anthropology in Micronesia. Applied Anthropology. 6(4):1-14.

129-133 ANTHROPOLOGY IN USE

129   BELGIUM   1947

   The Belgium government created IRSAC (Institute pour la Recherche Scientifique en Afrique Centrale) to organize anthropological research efforts in the Belgian Congo and Ruanda-Urundi.

   Richards, Audrey I.
   1953   Africa, South of Sahara. In International Directory of Anthropological Institutions. William L. Thomas, Jr. and Anna M. Pikelis (eds.). New York: Wenner-Gren.

130   BECHUANALAND   1947

   Schapera's publication, Migrant Labour and Tribal Life, reported research carried out at the request of the colonial government and included a significant number of policy recommendations.

   Schapera, Isaac
   1947   Migrant Labour and Tribal Life. London: Oxford University Press.

131   UNITED STATES   1947

   The Advisory Committee on Education for Guam and the Trust Territory, initiated by the U.S. Navy, was established.

   Society for Applied Anthropology
   1949   People and Project. Human Organization. 8(2):25-28.

132   UNITED STATES   1948

   Felix M. Kessing was appointed Senior Commissioner for the United States of the South Pacific Commission. The commission was advised by a research council which had anthropologists as members.

   American Anthropological Association
   1955   News of Councils, Foundations and Societies. Bulletin, American Anthropological Association. 3(1):9-10.

133   UNITED STATES   1948

   The initiation of the Fox Project, under the leadership of Sol Tax, used an approach called "action anthropology" and represents one of the first value-explicit approaches. Its goal was to bring about changes in an American Indian community in Iowa and its relationships with nearby white communities. The project had associated scientific goals. This is one of the earliest of the intervention techniques developed in anthropology.

   Diesing, Paul
   1960   A Method of Social Problem Solving. In Documentary History of the Fox Project. Department of Anthropology, University of Chicago.

Gearing, Frederick
1960   The Strategy of the Fox Project. In Documentary History
         of the Fox Project. Department of Anthropology,
         University of Chicago.

Gearing, Frederick, Robert Mc.Netting and Lisa R. Peattie
1960   Documentary History of the Fox Project. Department
         of Anthropology, University of Chicago.

Peattie, Lisa R.
1960   The Failure of the Means-Ends Scheme in Action Anthro-
         pology. In Documentary History of the Fox Project.
         Department of Anthropology, University of Chicago.

Piddington, Ralph
1960   Action Anthropology. Journal of the Polynesian Society.
         69:199-213.

Tax, Sol
1958   The Fox Project. Human Organization. 17:17-19.

1960   Action Anthropology. In Documentary History of the
         Fox Project. Department of Anthropology, University
         of Chicago.

134   UNITED STATES   1948

      A Boston preventative psychiatry group, the Human Relations Service,
      was established. David F. Aberle served as a staff member researching
      family cases. This represents an early appearance of the anthropo-
      logist working in conjunction with a clinic.

      Aberle, David F.
      1950   Introducing Preventative Psychiatry into a Community.
               Human Organization. 9(3):5-9.

135   INDIA   1948

      An assessment of the Madras state education program was carried
      out by anthropologist A. Aiyappan who submitted a report with
      recommendations to the Government of Madras.

      Aiyappan, A.
      1948   Report on the Socio-Economic Condition of Aboriginal
               Tribes of Madras. Madras.

136   MEXICO   1948

      National Indian Institute was founded to carry out research and
      development activities among the indigeneous population of Mexico.
      Anthropologists worked in various administrative contexts.

      Caso, Alfonso
      1958   Ideals of an Action Program. Human Organization.
               17(1):27-29.

de la Fuente, Julio
1958   National Indigenous Institute of Mexico: A Report-
         Results of an Action Program. Human Organization.
         17(1):30-33.

Huizer, Gerrit
1968   Community Development and Conflicting Rural Interests,
         Some Observations on the Programme of the National
         Indian Institute in Mexico. American Indigena.
         28(3):619-629.

Instituto Indigenista Interamericano
1948   Creation of the National Indian Institute. Boletin
         Indigenista. 8(3-4):259-63.

137 MICRONESIA   1948

The Navy Department hired staff anthropologists for work in
Micronesia. Anthropologists were later hired by the civilian
administration. They tended to be placed in staff as opposed to
line positions.

Barnett, H. G.
1956   Anthropology in Administration. Evanston, Illinois:
         Row, Peterson.

Criswell, John H.
1958   Anthropology and the Navy. In Anthropology in the Armed
         Services: Research in Environment, Physique and Social
         Organization. L. Dupree (ed.). University Park, Pa.:
         Pennsylvania State University, Social Science Research
         Center.

Drucker, Philip
1951   Anthropology in the Trust Territory. The Scientific
         Monthly. 72(5).

Solenberger, R. R.
1964   Continuity of Local Political Institutions in the
         Marianas. Human Organization. 23(1):53-60.

Useem, John
1945   Governing the Occupied Areas of the South Pacific:
         Wartime Lessons and Peace Time Proposals. Applied
         Anthropology. 4(3):1-10.

138 INDIA   1948

The community development approach to rural development was
applied on a pilot basis to a region of the North Indian state
of Uttar Pradesh. The group which designed the original program
was led by town planner Albert Mayer. The team was assisted by
various social scientists including anthropologists McKim Marriott

and Rudra Datt Singh. This project became the model for the national program of community development.

Mayer, Albert with M. Marriott and R. L. Park
1958   Pilot Project, India, the Story of Rural Development at Etawah, Uttar Pradesh. Berkeley: University of California Press.

139   UNITED STATES   1948

One of the many significant applied anthropology projects in which Cornell University anthropologists came to be involved was the Southwestern Field Station Project at Fruitland, New Mexico. The activities of the project were predominantly research focused, primarily on an evaluation of the Fruitland irrigation project. The Fruitland project was initiated some eight years earlier by the Bureau of Indian Affairs to provide irrigated farm land to Navajo Indians. The working agreement between the BIA and the Cornell group called for the determination of the social effects of the various development efforts and making of recommendations for subsequent efforts. The anthropologists involved included Tom T. Sasaki, John Adair, Alexander Leighton, Clifford Barnett, and Milton Barnett.

Sasaki, Tom T.
1960   Fruitland, New Mexico: A Navaho Community in Transition. Ithaca, New York: Cornell University Press.

Sasaki, Tom T. and John Adair
1952   New Land to Farm: Agricultural Practices Among the Navaho Indians of New Mexico. In Human Problems in Technological Change. Edward H. Spicer (ed.). New York: Russell Sage.

140   MEXICO   1948

The Instituto Nacional Indigenista was founded. Staffed largely by anthropologists, I.N.I. came to bear a major responsibility in the education and development of the native population of Mexico through its coordinating centers. The role of anthropologists was sharply reduced in the 1970s.

Comas, Juan
1953   Mexico. In International Directory of Anthropological Institutions. Thomas and Pikelis (eds.). New York: Wenner-Gren Foundation.

141   MICRONESIA   1948

The establishment of the Scientific Investigations in Micronesia or SIM project was sponsored by the Pacific Science Board and financed by the Office of Naval Research. SIM replaced CIMA, (Coordinated Investigation of Micronesian Anthropology). The primary focus of SIM was the Coral Atoll Project which used a multidisciplinary team approach to research the ecology of various atolls. The islands of Arno (Marshalls), Onotoa (Gilberts), Raroia (Tuamotus), and Ifaluk (Western Carolines) were studied.

Barnett, Homer G.
1956   Anthropology in Administration. Evanston: Row, Peterson.

Pacific Science Board
1951   Fifth Annual Report, Pacific Science Board, National Research Council. Washington: National Research Council.

142 MICRONESIA   1948

Emergency investigation into the causes of and solutions to the problems associated with the forced relocation of the Bikini atoll population to Rongerik was started. The Bikinians were forced to relocate because their home atoll was selected as an atomic test site in 1946. The move caused traumatic effects.

Kiste, Robert C.
1974   The Bikinians: A Study in Forced Migration. Menlo Park: Cummings Publishing Company.

Mason, Leonard
1950   The Bikinians: A Transplanted Population. Human Organization. 9(1):5-15.

1958   Kili Community in Transition. South Pacific Commission Quarterly Bulletin. 18:32-35.

143 UNITED STATES   1948

The South Pacific Commission Research Council, sponsored by various governments, provided recommendations concerning research needs of the Southern Pacific and published scholarly material.

South Pacific Commission
1951   Report of the South Pacific Commission for the Year 1950. Nonmea, New Caledonia: South Pacific Commission.

144 FRANCE   1949

The United Nations Economic Scientific and Cultural Council convened a scientific board in Paris, "to consider the desirability of initiating and recommending the general adoption of a program of disseminating scientific facts designed to remove what is generally known as racial prejudice" (UNESCO 1961:493-494). A Declaration of Race was issued in 1950. This statement was developed by a group which included anthropologists.

Comas, Juan
1978 The International Fight Against Racism: Words and Realities. Human Organization. 37(4):334-344.

UNESCO
1961 Race and Science. The Race Question in Modern Science. New York: Columbia University Press.

145 FRANCE   1949

Anthropologists participated in early UNESCO attempts to develop the Universal Declaration of Human Rights.

Metraux, Alfred
1951 UNESCO and Anthropology. American Anthropologist. 53(2):294-300.

1953 Applied Anthropology in Government: United Nations. In Anthropology Today. A. L. Kroeber (ed.). Chicago: University of Chicago Press.

146 UNITED STATES   1949

The Society for Applied Anthropology published their first Code of Ethics. The process by which an ethics code was developed began in 1946. After much discussion, the committee's report was published in the Society's newly renamed journal, **Human Organization**. The ethics code has been subsequently changed. This appears to be the first ethics code published by a professional association in anthropology.

Mead, Margaret, Eliot D. Chapple and G. Gordon Brown
1949 Report of the Committee on Ethics. Human Organization. 8(2):20-21.

147 UNITED STATES   1949

The Missouri River Basin Investigations Staff was created. The group was to research the impact of water resources development.

Cushman, Frances and Gordon MacGregor
1949 Harnessing the Big Muddy. Lawrence Kansas: Indian Service.

MacGregor, Gordon
1949 Attitudes of the Fort Berthold Indians Regarding Removal from the Garrison Reservoir Site and Future Administration of their Reservation. North Dakota History. 16(1).

148 JAPAN   1949

American anthropologists participated in the occupation of Japan following the treaty. These included John W. Bennett who was employed as Chief of the Public Opinion of Civil Information and

Education Section of the Supreme Commander Allied Powers and Robert B. Textor who was Assistant Civil Information and Education Officer for I Corps at Kyoto. Bennett engaged in a number of research efforts including attempts to assess the effects of the land reform program.

Bennett, John W. and Ishino Iwao
1955 Futomi: A Case Study of the Socio-Economic Adjustments of a Marginal Community in Japan. Rural Sociology. 20:41-50.

Bennett, John W.
1951 Community Research in the Japan Occupation. Clearinghouse Bulletin of Research in Human Organization. 1(3):1-5.

1952 Social and Attitudinal Research in Japan: The Work of SCAP's Public Opinion and Sociological Research (PO and SR) Division. Journal of East Asiatic Studies (Manila). 2(1):21-33.

Ishino, Iwao
1956 Motivational Factors in a Japanese Labor Supply Organization. Human Organization. 15(1):12-17.

Bennett, John W. and Ishino Iwao
1963 Paternalism in the Japanese Economy: Anthropological Studies of Oyabun-Kobun Patterns. Minneapolis: University of Minnesota Press.

Textor, Robert B.
1951 Failure in Japan. New York: John Day Company.

149 UNITED STATES 1950

Robert Redfield served as an expert witness in Sweatt v Painter, as it was argued before the United States Supreme Court. This case, which dealt with a legal attack on segregated law school facilities at the University of Texas anticipated Brown v Board of Education. Redfield indicated that no rational foundation for segregation was to be found in the social science literature.

Kluger, Richard
1976 Simple Justice: The History of Brown v Board of Education and Black America's Struggle for Equality. New York: Knopf.

150 MICRONESIA 1950

Anthropologists were hired by the U.S. Navy to serve on the staff of civil administration on Palau, Truk, the Marshalls, Ponape, and Yap.

Barnett, Homer G.
1956 Anthropology in Administration. Evanston: Harper, Row.

Drucker, Philip
1951   Anthropology in Trust Territory Administration. The
        Scientific Monthly. 72(5).

151 UNITED STATES   1950

    The Technical Cooperation Administration of the U.S. Department
    of State was established. This organization hired anthropologists.

    Voegelin, Erminie W.
    1953   United States. In International Directory of Anthropolo-
            gical Institutions. William L. Thomas, Jr. and Anna M.
            Pikelis (eds.).

152 CANADA   1950

    The inquiry into the causes of disturbances in Doukhobor communities
    in British Columbia was carried out by a research team which included
    an anthropologist. Project efforts included the formation of a
    committee which facilitated mediation between the Doukhobors and
    the provincial government.

    Hawthorn, Harry B. (ed.)
    1952   The Doukhobors of British Columbia, Report of the
            Doukhobors Research Committee. University of British
            Columbia.

153 MICRONESIA   1950

    A survey of conditions in Micronesia was made in anticipation of
    the administrative transfer from Naval administration to the
    United States Department of Interior.

    Department of the Interior
    1951   Management Survey of the Government of the Trust Territory
            of the Pacific Islands. Washington, D.C.: Office of
            Territories, Department of the Interior.

154 UNITED STATES   1951

    The American Anthropological Association sponsored the preparation
    of, "Intercultural Transfer of Techniques, A Manual of Applied
    Social Science for Point IV Technicians and Administrators Overseas."
    This was later published for the general public under the title
    Introducing Social Change.

    Arensberg, Conrad M. and Arthur H. Niehoff
    1964   Introducing Social Change, A Manual for Americans
            Overseas. Chicago: Aldine Publishing.

155 UNITED STATES   1951

    The Human Resources Research Center at Randolph AFB, San Antonio,

Texas, hired anthropologists Alan R. Beals and Walter Goldschmidt to use participant-observation research techniques to identify factors related to B-29 bomber crew efficiency. The research focused upon three issues, these include; the crew formation process, the effect of the aircraft on the crew as social unit and the relations between the crew and the rest of the Air Force. The research produced reports which were in the end supressed.

Beals, Alan R.
1976   Flying the Big'uns: Ethnography of a B-29 Crew. In Paths to the Symbolic Self, Essays in Honor of Walter Goldschmidt. J. P. Loucky and J. R. Jones (eds.). Anthropology, UCLA. 8(1 and 2).

156   UNITED STATES   1951

Various anthropologists provided testimony in a number of trials dealing with the use and possession of peyote by members of the Native American Church. The case was based on the view that peyote was sacramental in nature and its use should be allowed on Constitutional grounds.

La Barre, Weston, David P. McAllester, J. S. Slotkin, Omer C. Stewart and Sol Tax
1951   Statement on Peyote.• Science. 114:582-583.

157   UNITED STATES   1951

Staff members of the Institute of Social Anthropology, Smithsonian Institution, carried out research projects which evaluated various United States government technical assistance projects in Brazil, Columbia, Mexico, and Peru. Field analyses were carried out by Charles Erasmus, Isabel Kelly, Kalervo Oberg, George Foster, and Ozzie Simmons.

Foster, George
1951   A Cross-Cultural Anthropological Analysis of a Technical Aid Program. Washington: Institute of Social Anthropology, Smithsonian Institution.

Kelly, Isabel
1960   La Anthropologia, la Cultura y la Salud Publica. Lima: Ministry de Salud Publica y A.S.

158   GREAT BRITAIN   1951

Raymond Firth evaluated the so-called Colombo Plan which intended to reform British colonial administration and accelerate colonial development. Firth warned of unforeseen social consequences.

Firth, Raymond W.
1951   Some Social Aspects of the Colombo Plan. Westminster Bank Review (May).

Mair, Lucy
1969   Applied Anthropology and Development Policies in Anthropology and Social Change. London School of Economics, Monographs on Social Anthropology, No. 38 New York: Humanities Press.

159   GAUTEMALA   1951

The Institute of Nutrition of Central America and Panama (INCAP) sponsored research to discover a means for overcoming resistance to INCAP projects in a predominantly Indian community. An anthropologist was engaged to research the problem and identified a number of causes. These included defects in communication, political conflict between factions, a counter-productive social welfare program and an array of conflict-generating contrasts between local custom and introduced practices in the realm of health beliefs.

Adams, Richard N.
1952   La Antropologia Applicada en Los Programas de Salud Pública de la América Latina. Boletin de la Oficina Sanitaria Panamericana, 33(4):298-305.

1953   Notes on the Application of Anthropology. Human Organization. 12(2):10-14.

160   NORTHERN RHODESIA   1951

As part of an attempt to provide relevant information to "public authorities" concerning urbanization and urban life in Rhodesia the Rhodes-Livingstone Institute carried out surveys of urban dwellers to determine some basic demographic characteristics. The director of the survey was J. Clyde Mitchell.

Mitchell, J. Clyde
1954   African Urbanization in Ndola and Luanshya. Rhodes-Livingstone Communication Number Six, Lusaka: Rhodes-Livingstone Institute.

161   UNITED STATES   1951

A group of citizens from Talladega, Alabama, approached the University of Alabama to find out the range of health services that might be available to them. This inquiry led to a research group being formed at the University which developed a working relationship with the Talladega community. The research group for the most part limited its activites to research, but did consult on various problems. During the two years of the project, a community council was formed, a health inventory and various development projects were carried out. Anthropologists in the project included Asael T. Hansen, Solon T. Kimball, and Marion Pearsall.

Kimball, Solon T.
1952   Some Methodological Problems of the Community Self-Survey. Social Forces. 31:160-164.

162–164 ANTHROPOLOGY IN USE

1955   An Alabama Town Surveys its Health Needs. In Health Culture and Community. B. D. Paul (ed.). New York: Russell Sage.

Kimball, Solon T. and Marion Pearsall
1954   The Talladega Story, A Study in Community Process. University, Alabama: University of Alabama Press.

Pearsall, Marion
1955   Community Self-Surveys and Mental Health Programs. Alabama Mental Health. 7:1-3.

162   FRANCE   1951

UNESCO convened a second conference on racism to improve the document titled "A Declaration on Race and Racial Differences" published in 1950.

Ashely-Montagu, M. F.
1951   Statement on Race. An Extended Discussion in Plain Language of the UNESCO Statement by Experts on Race Problems. New York: Henry Shuman.

Comas, Juan
1978   The International Fight Against Racism: Words and Realities. Human Organization. 37(4):334-344.

163   AMERICAN SAMOA   1951

Samoan Affairs Officer position was created to advise the American civilian government on native affairs. The position was to be filled by a cultural anthropologist.

MacGregor, Gordon
1955   Anthropology in Government: United States. In Yearbook of Anthropology, 1955, William L. Thomas, (ed.). New York: Wenner-Gren.

164   UNITED STATES   1951

Anthropologists and other behavioral scientists were hired to assist I.C.A. programs overseas. I.C.A., or the International Cooperation Administration, became known as A.I.D. in 1961. Anthropologists served both as administrators and "community analysts."

Boggs, Stephen T.
1960   The Organization of Anthropology in Action. Human Organization. 23(3):193-195.

Galdwin, Thomas
1960   Technical Assistance Programs: A Challenge for Anthropology, Fellow Newsletter, American Anthropological Association, 1(10):6-7.

Hamilton, James W.
1973   Problems in Government Anthropology in Anthropology Beyond
        the University, Proceedings of the Southern Anthropological
        Society, No. 7, A. Redfield, (ed.). Athens: University of
        Georgia Press.

Kelly, Isabel
1956   Anthropological Approach to Midwifery Training in Mexico.
        Journal of Tropical Pediatrics, 1:200-205.

1959   Technical Cooperation and the Culture of the Host Community.
        Community Development Review. (September 1959).

1964   Suggestions for the Training of Village-Level Workers,
        Human Organization, 21(4):241-245.

Miniclier, Louis
1964   The Use of Anthropologists in the Foreign Aid Program.
        Human Organization. 23(3):187-189.

Schaedel, Richard P.
1964   Anthropology in AID Overseas Missions: Its Practical and
        Theoretical Potential. Human Organization, 23(3):190-192.

165 BRITISH SOLOMONS (TIKOPIA)   1952

In response to conditions of famine caused by a hurricane, anthropologists James Spillius and Raymond Firth developed an applied
approach in the field to better assist the Tikopia. The approach
was value-explicit and suggests elements of both cultural brokerage
and participant intervention. This represents one of few examples
of involvement in the action by "British" social anthropologists.
The dimensions of role are dealt with explicitly.

Spillius, James
1957   Natural Disaster and Political Crisis in a Polynesian
        Society: An Exploration of Operational Research II.
        Human Relations. X(2):113-125.

166 UNITED STATES   1952

A. L. Kroeber was retained as expert witness by the attorneys for
"Indians of California" in their case before the Indian Claims Com-
mission. Kroeber worked in this endeavor with the assistance of
Robert F. Heizer, Edward W. Gifford, Samuel A. Barrett, S. F. Cook
and Donald Cutter. Kroeber developed an up-dated linguistic map of
California for his testimony. The Handbook of California Indians
produced by Kroeber was used in evidence. The government hired
anthropologists to support their case. These persons included Julian
H. Steward, William D. Strong, Harold Driver, Erminie Voegelin, Walter
R. Goldschmidt, Abraham Halpern, and Ralph L. Beals. The government's argument suggested that the native population of California
exploited a narrow range of ecological opportunities.

Stewart, Omer C.
1961   Kroeber and the Indian Claims Commission Cases. Kroeber Anthropological Society Paper No. 25 Alfred L. Kroeber, a memorium.

167   SUDAN   1952

The Zande Scheme was based on proposals developed by J. D. Tothill for the development of agriculture in British Africa. The ultimate goal was the creation of, "happy, prosperous, literate communities, based on agriculture and participating in the benefits of civilization." The area in which the Azande lived in southern Sudan was selected as a pilot area. Conrad C. Reining carried out research to determine the effects of the project with the financial support of the government of Anglo-Egyptian Sudan.

Reining, Conrad C.
1966   The Zande Scheme, An Anthropological Case Study of Economic Development in Africa. Evanston: Northwestern University Press.

168   PERU   1952

Under the leadership of Allan R. Holmberg, the Cornell-Vicos project attempted to bring about political and economic change in a community in highland Peru. The approach used is termed "research and development" anthropology. It is one of the first systematic value-explicit approaches. The approach developed at Vicos was applied in a number of other contexts. The project had a significant research output and is very well documented.

Alers, J. Oscar
1965   The Question of Well-being. American Behavioral Scientist, 8(7):18-22.

Alers, J. Oscar, Mario C. Vasquez, Allan R. Holmberg, and Henry F. Dobyns
1965   Human Freedom and Geographic Mobility. Current Anthropology, 6(3):336.

Collier, John and Mary Collier
1957   An Experiment in Applied Anthropology. Scientific American. 196(1):37-45.

Dobyns, Henry F.
1965   The Strategic Importance of Enlightenment and Skill for Power. American Behavioral Scientist. 8(7):23.

Dobyns, Henry F., Paul L. Doughty and Harold D. Lasswell
1971   Peasants, Power, and Applied Social Change, Vicos as a Model. Beverly Hills: Sage.

Dobyns, Henry F., Carlos Monge M. and Mario C. Vasquez
1962   A Contagious Experiment: the Vicos Idea Has Spread Throughout Peru. Saturday Review. (November 3, 1962) pp. 59-62.

Doughty, Paul L.
1965   The Interrelationship of Power, Respect, Affection and Rectitude in Vicos. American Behavioral Scientist, 8(7):13-17.

Freid, Jacob
1962   Social Organization and Personal Security in a Peruvian Hacienda Indian Community: Vicos. American Anthropologist. 64(4):771.

Holmberg, Allan R.
1954   Participant Intervention in the Field. Human Organization. 14(1):23-26.

1956   From Paternalism to Democracy: Cornell Peru Project. Human Organization, 15(3):15-18.

1958   The Research and Development Approach to the Study of Culture Change. Human Organization. 17(1):12-16.

1959   Land Tenure and Planned Social Change: A Case from Vicos, Peru. Human Organization, 18(1):7-10.

1965   The Changing Values and Institutions of Vicos in the Context of National Development. American Behavioral Scientist. 8(7):3-8.

1966   Vicos: Metodo y Practica de Antropologia Aplicada, (Investigaciones Sociales, Serie: Monografias Andinas, No. 5). Lima: Editorial Estudios Andinos, S. A.

Holmberg, Allan R. and Henry F. Dobyns
1962   The Process of Accelerating Community Change. Human Organization. 21(2):107-109.

Holmberg, Allan R., Henry F. Dobyns and Mario C. Vasquez
1961   Methods for the Analysis of Culture Change, Anthropological Quarterly. 34(2):37-46.

Huizer, Gerritt
1972   Overcoming Resistance to Change: The Vicos Experiment, in The Revolutionary Potential of Peasants in Latin America. Lexington, MA: D. C. Heath.

Lasswell, Harold D.
1962   Integrating Communities into More Inclusive Systems. Human Organization. 21(2):116-121.

Lear, John
1962   Reaching the Heart of South America, Saturday Review. (November 3rd. 1962) pp. 55-58.

Newman, Marshall T., Carlos Collazos Chiriboga and Carmen de Fuentes
1963   Growth differences between Indians and Mestizos in the Callejon de Huaylas, Peru. American Journal of Physical Anthropology. 21:407-408.

1963   Physical and Clinical Changes in Vicos Indian Boys with Improved Dietary Status, American Journal of Physical Anthropology. 21.

Vazquez, Mario C.
1952   La Antropologia Cultural y Nuestro Problema del Indio: Vicos, un Caso de Antropologia Aplicada. Peru Indigena. 2:5-157.

1965   The Interplay between Power and Wealth. American Behavioral Scientist. 8:9-12.

Vazquez, Mario C. and Allan R. Holmberg
1966   The Castas: Unilineal Kin Groups in Vicos, Peru. Cornell University, Department of Anthropology

169   UNITED STATES   1952

Anthropologists participated in the evaluation of the Latin American Health Development programs of the Institute of Inter-American Affairs. The Institute was a United States Government venture. The team which evaluated the broad spectrum ten year project included a number of anthropologists; George M. Foster (El Salvador and Chile), Charles Erasmus (Columbia and Ecuador), Isabel T. Kelly (Mexico), Kalervo Oberg (Brazil), and Ozzie Simmons (Peru and Chile).

Foster, George M.
1953   Use of Anthropological Methods and Data in Planning and Operation. Public Health Reports, 68(9):841-857.

1976   Medical Anthropology and International Health Planning. Medical Anthropology Newsletter, 7(3):12-18.

170   UNITED STATES   1952

Application of action-anthropology techniques in urban redevelopment areas of South-side Chicago began when Sol Tax, participating in his own community, implemented the technique developed with the Fox. The goal of the project was neighborhood integration and continuity. Tax suggests that the experiences in Chicago as a citizen influenced his activities in Iowa as anthropologist.

Tax, Sol
1959   Residential Integration: The Case of Hyde Park in
        Chicago. Human Organization. 18(1):22-27.

171 UNITED STATES   1952

Human Problems in Technological Change, A Casebook was published
by the Russell Sage Foundation. Based on a conception of Alexander
H. Leighton, the book developed from Cornell University seminars in
applied anthropology and consisted of various case studies.

Spicer, Edward H. (ed.)
1952   Human Problems in Technological Change. New York: Russell
        Sage Foundation.

172 MEXICO   1952

Following the Papaloapan project, a similar project was initiated in
the Tepalcatepec basin. The staff anthropologist, Aguirre Beltran,
researched the region which was inhabited by 256,000 persons.

Beltran, Aguirre
1952   Problemas de la Poblacion Indigena de la Cuenca del
        Tepalcatepec. Memorias de I.N.I. III.

173 INDIA   1952

Oscar Lewis was hired as a consultant for the Ford Foundation in
India. He was requested to work with the Program Evaluation
Organization of the Planning Commission to review a plan of evaluation of the rural reconstruction program. This program served as
a pilot for community development in India.

Lewis, Oscar
1958   Village Life in Northern India. New York: Vintage.

174 UNITED STATES   1952

George Spindler developed an approach referred to as "cultural
therapy." Used with a school principal Spindler successfully increased the principal's capacity for dealing with persons with different cultural identities. This process involved presenting the
principal with data concerning his own cultural background and the
nature of his selective response to students over a period of time.
Spindler was able to increase the person's "cultural scope."

Prieto, A. G.
1957   American Education--The Image in the Mirror. Reviews in
        Anthropology. 2(2):286-290.

Spindler, G. D.
1959   The Transmission of American Culture. Cambridge, Mass.:
        Harvard University Press.

175–178 ANTHROPOLOGY IN USE

1974   Cultural Sensitization. In Education and Cultural Process: Toward an Anthropology of Education. G. Spindler (ed.). New York: Holt, Rinehart and Winston.

175   PAKISTAN   1952

American anthropologist John J. Honigman was hired by an agency of the U. S. Department of State to evaluate the effects of U. S. information films on rural audiences. Honigman concentrated his efforts on three villages in different linguistic areas of what was then West Pakistan.

Honigman, John J.
1953   Information for Pakistan, Report of Research on Intercultural Communication through Films. Chapel Hill: Institute for Research in Social Science, University of North Carolina.

176   UNITED STATES   1953

Anthropologists studied the human environment in the region around the Arctic Research Laboratory of the Navy at Point Barrow, Alaska. The Navy was concerned about the long term impact on Eskimos of employment at the Naval Petroleum Reserve IV base. The anthropologist concluded that the Eskimo would be able to return to their previous economic pattern if employment opportunities at the base declined.

Criswell, Joan H.
1958   Anthropology and the Navy. In Anthropology in the Armed Services, Research in Environment, Physique, and Social Organization. Louis Dupree (ed.). University Park, PA: Pennsylvania State University Social Science Research Center.

177   UNITED STATES   1953

A Branch of the Foreign Service Institute was established at the American Embassy in Lebanon for the training of younger foreign service officers being posted to the Middle East. The Institute staff included anthropologist Kepler Lewis and linguist Charles Ferguson.

McGregor, Gordon
1955   Anthropology in Government: United States. In Yearbook of Anthropology, 1955. William L. Thomas, Jr., (ed.). New York: Wenner-Gren.

178   UNITED STATES   1953

The Mutual Security Administration of the United States used social scientists, including anthropologists, to study their various programs in Southeast Asia.

McNamara, Robert L.
1953   The Role of a Social Science Adviser to a STEM Mission.
        Economic Development and Culture Change, (5):390-393.

179 UNITED STATES   1953

Elmer R. Smith was invited to join the Utah State Department of
Education, Committee for the Revision of the State School Course
of Study in Human Relations. As an anthropologist, Smith was
expected to contribute to a better curriculum in the area of inter-
ethnic relations.

Hoebel, E. Adamson
1955   Anthropology in Education. In Yearbook of Anthropology,
        1955. New York: Wenner-Gren Foundation.

180 UNITED STATES   1954

In a talk to an American wives club in Rio de Janeiro, Brazil,
Kalvero Oberg presented the concept of Culture Shock, a label he
created for the common expatriate and foreign traveler syndrome.
The concept came to be very significant in terms of training for
foreign travel, study and work.

Oberg, Kalvero
1954   Culture Shock. Bobbs-Merrill Reprint Series in the Social
        Sciences, A-329.

181 UNITED STATES   1954

Some ethnohistorical and legal problems confronted by the plaintiffs,
defendants and attorneys were explored at a 1954 symposium on the
Indian Claims Act. The central problem seemed to be the determination
of the role of expert witness that fulfilled the specific needs of
the Department of Justice and was an acceptable role extension for
anthropologists. Participants were Ralph A. Barney, Chief of the
Indian Claims Section, Lands Division, Department of Justice; Donald
C. Gormley of the law firm of Wilkinson, Boyden, Cragun and Barker;
and anthropologists Verne Ray, Julian Steward, A. L. Kroeber, J.A.
Jones, and Nancy Oestreich Lurie. An excellent discussion of the
expert witness role is provided by Dobyns (1978).

Barney, Ralph A.
1955   Legal Problems Peculiar to Indian Claims Litigation.
        Ethnohistory. 2(1):315-325.

Dobyns, Henry F.
1978   Taking the Witness Stand. In Applied Anthropology in
        America. E. M. Eddy and W. L. Partridge (eds.). New York:
        Columbia University Press.

Jones, J. A.
1955   Anthropology and Indian Claims Litigation: Problems,
        Opportunities and Recommendations. Ethnohistory,
        2(1):347-356.

Kroeber, A. L.
1955   The Nature of the Land Holding Group. Ethnohistory, 2(1):303-314.

Lurie, Nancy Oestreich
1955   Problems, Opportunities, and Recommendations, Ethnohistory 2(1):357-375.

Ray, Verne F.
1955   Introduction to Indian Claims Litigation, Ethnohistory, 2(1):277-292.

Steward, Julian H.
1955   Theory and Application in a Social Science, Ethnohistory 2(1):292-302.

182   NETHERLANDS   1954

Anthropologist J. W. Schoorl was assigned by the Governor of West Irian to carry out a research project in the Muyu region of that country. Schoorl, prior to this had served the Dutch Colonial service for two years. The research focused on various "administrative problems" such as the government's system of licensing "pig feast," the practices associated with witchcraft, and the policy toward cowry money. Schoorl made policy recommendations as part of his study.

Schoorl, J. W.
1967   The Anthropologist in Government Service. In Anthropologists in the Field. D. G. Jongmans and P. C. W. Gutkind, (eds.). Assen: Van Gorcum.

183   INDIA   1954

Verrier Elwin was appointed advisor for Tribal Affairs by the North-East Frontier Agency. The efforts in N.E.F.A. were coupled with basic ethnography research programs.

Fuchs, Stephen
1969   Applied Anthropology in India. In Anthropology and Archaeology, Essays in Commemoration of Verrier Elwin. M. C. Pradhan, R. D. Singh, P. K. Misra, and D. B. Sastry, (eds.). London: Oxford University Press.

184   UNITED STATES   1955

The Navajo-Cornell Field Health Project at Many Farms, Arizona, represented an early, sophisticated attempt to improve the quality of western health care delivery to a non-western population through the cooperative research and development efforts of a team of anthropologists and health care professionals. The project was carried out with the cooperation of the Navajo Tribal Government and the United States Public Health Service.

Adair, John
1960   The Indian Health Worker in the Cornell-Navaho Project.
        Human Organization. 19(2):59-63.

Deuschle, Kurt, John Adair and Hugh Fulmer
1958   The Navajo-Cornell Health Research Project at Many Farms.
        In Navajo Yearbook, Report No. VII. Window Rock, AR:
        Navajo Agency

Richards, Cara E.
1960   Cooperation Between Anthropologists and Medical Personnel,
        Human Organization, 19:64-67.

Rabin, David L., et al
1965   Untreated Congenital Hip Disease: A Study of the
        Epidemiology, Natural History, and Social Aspects of
        the Disease in a Navajo Population, American Journal of
        of Public Health, 55(2) Supplement.

185 NORTHERN RHODESIA   1955

The African Railway Workers Union requested that the Rhodes-Livingstone
Institute make a study of the organization of the union. The project
was carried out by Parkinson Mwewa in association with A. L. Epstein.

Mwewa, Parkinson B.
1958   The African Railway Workers Union Ndola, Northern Rhodesia.
        (Rhodes-Livingstone Communication Number Ten). Lusaka:
        Rhodes-Livingstone Institute.

186 UNITED NATIONS   1955

Cultural Patterns and Technical Change was published by the United
Nations Educational, Scientific and Cultural Organization. Edited
by Margaret Mead, it was intended for use by technicians, policy-
makers and others actively engaged in change agentry in cross-
cultural settings. Generally it is focused on the question, "How
can technical change be introduced with such regard for culture
pattern that human values are preserved?" (Mead, 1955)

Mead, Margaret, ed.
1955   Cultural Patterns and Technical Change, New York: Mentor.

187 UNITED STATES   1955

Anthropologist Louis Miniclier's organization of three "Teams"
reviewed early community development in such countries as India,
Pakistan, Philippines, Egypt, the Gold Coast, Puerto Rico and others.
George Foster headed up one team, Isabel Kelly another.

188–190 ANTHROPOLOGY IN USE

Adams, Harold S., George M. Foster and Paul S. Taylor
1955   Report on Community Development Programs in India, Pakistan and the Philippines. Washington, D. C.: International Cooperation Administration.

Carley, Verna A. and Elmer A. Starch
1956   Report on Community Development Programs in Jamaica, Puerto Rico, Bolivia and Peru. Washington, D. C.: International Cooperation Administration.

188   UNITED STATES   1955

The Wisconsin Legislative Council's Menominee Indian Study Committee, which investigated the impact of "Termination" on the Menominees, included anthropologists.

Ames, David W. and Burton R. Fisher
1959   The Menominee Termination Crisis: Barriers in the Way of a Rapid Cultural Transition. Human Organization, 18(2):101-111.

Lurie, Nancy O.
1972   Menominee Termination: From Reservation to Colony. Human Organization. 31(3).

189   UNITED STATES   1956

The Rehabilitation Project of the Massachusetts Mental Health Center made use of a culture based therapy strategy. The project, which focused on a halfway house for mentally ill women, viewed the rehabilitation process in terms of socialization into society at large. Although the therapy was based on anthropological theory, it was administered by a social worker. An anthropologist was attached to the project as a researcher.

Landy, David
1961   A Halfway House for Women; Preliminary Report of a Study. In Mental Patients in Transaction. Springfield: Charles C. Thomas.

190   UNITED STATES   1956

Using participant-observation techniques anthropologist Louis Dupree evaluated U. S. Air Force Bailed-out Crew Survival Systems. These evaluations were carried out in Panamanian rain forests, Libyan deserts and off the coast of Puerto Rico. Test groups were randomly selected from B-52 crews, and accompanied by an anthropologist. Each day the observer recorded information on prepared data cards. This included information on physical condition, equipment use and improvision, leadership, morale and reactions to the environment. The results of the research revealed a number of significant deficiencies in Air Force survival training. The role of the group commander was revealed to be very important.

Dupree, Louis
1956   The Jungle Survival Field Test. Maxwell AFB, Alabama, ADTIC Publ. T-101.

1956   The Desert Survival Field Test. Maxwell AFB, Alabama, ADTIC Publ. D-104.

1958   The Water Survival Field Tests. Maxwell AFB, Alabama, ADTIC Publ. G-107.

191 UNITED STATES   1956

The United States Public Health Service as part of its program of tuberculosis treatment and control contracted with various hospitals in Seattle, Washington to provide treatment to Alaskan Natives. This required that individual patients be hospitalized far from home. In 1956 Margaret Lantis who was one of the few anthropologists working for P.H.S. on a direct-hire basis, was requested to study the problems of Eskimos hospitalized in Seattle.

Lantis, Margaret L. and Evelyn B. Hadaway
1957   How Three Seattle Tuberculosis Hospitals Have Met the Needs of Their Eskimo Patients. Paper presented to the National Tuberculosis Association, Kansas City, Missouri.

192 INDIA   1957

A policy guide for tribal peoples in the Northeast Frontier Agency was prepared by anthropologist Verrier Elwin. Elwin's position has been criticized as highly isolationist, although he denies this. The volume was supplemented by a "foreword" written by then Prime Minister Jawaharlal Nehru which contained Nehru's Five Principles for tribal people. The guide encouraged cultural pluralism.

Elwin, Verrier
1957   A Philosophy for NEFA. Shillong: Government of Assam.

Elwin, Verrier
1977   Growth of a 'Philosophy'. In Anthropology in the Development Process. H. N. Mathur (ed.). New Delhi: Vikas Publishing House.

193 MAURITIUS

One of the first anthropologists to assist organizations concerned with birth planning was Burton Benedict who was asked by the International Planned Parenthood Federation to give advice on how to implement the recommendations of the Committee on Population in Mauritius. Benedict went on to help set up the Mauritius Family Planning Association. He also served on the Royal Society Population Study Group from its founding in 1965 to 1968.

Benedict, Burton
1970   Controlling Population Growth in Mauritius. Paper presented to the meetings of the American Anthropological Association, San Diego.

194 SOUTHEAST ASIA   1957

The Mekong River Project was initiated by the establishment of the Committee for the Coordination of Investigations of the Lower Mekong Basin, under the auspices of the United Nations Economic Commission for the Far East and Asia (ECAFE). The plan involved the construction of a series of multiple purpose projects on the Mekong River which flows through Cambodia, Laos, Vietnam, and Thailand. Because the construction of dams on would affect lives of various ethnic groups in the region, anthropologists were actively involved in planning and evaluation of the planned projects.

Bardach, John E.
1972   Some Ecological Implications of Mekong River Development Plans. In the Careless Technology: Ecology and International Development. M. Taghi Farvar and John P. Milton (eds.). Garden City, N. Y.: The Natural History Press.

Ingersoll, Jasper
1968   Mekong River Basin Development: Anthropology in a New Setting. Anthropological Quarterly, 41:147-167.

1969   The Social Feasibility of PaMong Irrigation, A report to the U. S. Bureau of Reclamation and the U. S. Agency for International Development. Washington, D. C.

Solheim, Wilhelm
1961   The Importance of Anthropological Research to the Mekong Valley Project. France-Asia (Sept.-Oct.).

Halpern, Joel
1972a   Mekong River Development Schemes for Laos and Thailand. Internationales Asian Forum (Munich), Heft 1. Jahrgang 3, (Jan).

1972b   Some Reflections on the War in Laos, Anthropological or Otherwise. Centre d'Etude du Sud-Est Asiatique et de L'Extreme Orient. Brussels. Public mensuelle, 40 année, No. 44.

195 PHILIPPINES   1957

American anthropologist Harold C. Conklin began his substantial effort in Philippine ethnography in the period following the Second World War. This included work with the Hanunoo, a group on the island of Mindoro. While Conklin's work seems to have been intended to be basic research it did attract the attention of the Food and

Agriculture organization of the United Nations which published
Conklin's monograph on swidden or shifting agriculture of the
Hanunoo as part FAO's publication program focused upon shifting
cultivation. This was presented as a kind of policy-relevant
monograph. Marcel Leloup in his forword notes, "It will perhaps
come as a surprise to some readers that Dr. Conklin has not concluded his work by suggesting possible ways of improving the
standards of living of the group he has studied. It is felt,
however, that in this particular case there was no urgent need
for such suggestions. It is a case of almost perfect equilibrium
between man and his environment, and if there is any deterioration
on either side it is an extremely slow process " (1957:V).

The actual support for the research project came from the Social
Science Research Council and the Ford Foundation.

Conklin, Harold C.
1957   Hanunóo Agriculture, A Report on an Integral System of
        Shifting Cultivation in the Philippines   FAO Forestry
        Development Paper No. 12.

196   AFRICA

The African survey of Lord Hailey represents a massive effort
to collect data relevant to British colonial administration.

Hailey, W. H.
1958   An African Survey. London: Oxford.

Mair, Lucy
1960   The Social Sciences in Africa South of the Sahara:
        The British Contribution. Human Organization,
        19(3):98-107.

197   UNITED STATES   1958

By 1958 the U. S. Air Force had published 150 ethnic group guides
for downed air crew members. Each guide consists of a set of 5
by 8 inch cards which fit in a flight suit packet. Each set contains
information on population, range, environment, physical appearance,
language, religion, social organization, economy, diet, transportation
and tendency to be hostile. Most of the studies were prepared by
Air Force anthropologists.

Nesbitt, Paul H.
1958   Anthropology and the Air Force, Anthropology in the Armed
        Services: Research in Environment, Physique, and Social
        Organization. Louis Dupree (ed.) University Park, PA:
        Pennsylvania State University, Social Science Research Center.

198-201 ANTHROPOLOGY IN USE

198   PERU   1959

   The Kuyo Chico project was initiated as part of the National Program
   for the Integration of the Aboriginal Population of Peru. The project,
   which lasted until 1969, made use of the research and development
   technique, and, is an excellent example of a diverse anthropological
   role set. It was developed to bring about various economic, social,
   and political changes in an Indian community. The project was
   influenced by the Vicos project.

   Nunez Del Prado, Oscar with William Foote Whyte
   1973   Kuyo Chico: Applied Anthropology in an Indian Community.
             Chicago: University of Chicago Press.

199   UNITED STATES   1959

   Margaret Clark completed the first medical anthropology doctoral
   dissertation. George Foster served as her mentor.

   Clark, Margaret
   1959   Health in the Mexican-American Culture. Berkeley, CA:
             University of California Press.

200   INDIA   1960

   The Planning Commission of the government of India appointed a
   committee to evaluate the functioning of the so-called Multi-purpose
   Tribal Blocks. The committee was headed by anthropologist Verrier
   Elwin. Elwin's position on tribal affairs could be described as
   protectionist.

   Mathur, Hari Mohan
   1977   Anthropology, Government, and Developmental Planning, in
             India. In Anthropology in the Development Process. Hari
             Mohan Mathur (ed.). New Delhi: Vikas Publishing House.

   Elwin, Verrier
   1977   Growth of a 'Philosophy'. In Anthropology in the Develop-
             ment Process. Hari Mohan Mathur (ed.) New Delhi: Vikas
             Publishing House.

201   UNITED STATES   1960

   The Educational Resources in Anthropology (ERA) project, of the
   Department of Anthropology, University of California, Berkeley is
   significant for two reasons. First, it is an example of a general
   curriculum development project focused upon anthropology of various
   types and additionally it represents an early attempt to make
   recommendations on training in applied anthropology. Besides the
   various symposia which were held the project resulted in two rather

BIBLIOGRAPHIC CHRONOLOGY 201

substantial publications The Teaching of Anthropology and Resources for the Teaching of Anthropology published by the American Anthropological Association.

The recommendations on applied anthropology education are encompassed in three articles by Robert N. Rapoport, Laura Thompson, Kenneth Little, Homer G. Barnett and Richard N. Adams. Teaching anthropology to educators, public health specialists, and law students is also addressed.

While numerous specific recommendations are made, Mandelbaum points out that, "all five authors agree that there should be little difference between the training of an anthropologist who is going into an academic post and one who is preparing for work in the applied field" (1963:335).

Adams, Richard N.
1963   General Use of Studies in Applied Anthropology. In The Teaching of Anthropology. D. G. Mandelbaum et al (eds.). Memoir 94, Washington, D. C.: American Anthropological Association.

Barnett, Homer G.
1963   Materials for Course Design. In The Teaching of Anthropology. D. G. Mandelbaum, et al (eds.). Memoir 94, Washington, D.C. American Anthropological Association.

Hoebel, E. Adamson
1963   Anthropological Studies for Students of Law and Government. In The Teaching of Anthropology. D. G. Mandelbaum et al (eds.). Memoir 94, Washington, D. C.: American Anthropological Association.

Kimball, Solon T.
1963   Teaching Anthropology in Professional Education. In The Teaching of Anthropology. D. G. Mandelbaum et al (eds.). Memoir 94, Washington, D. C. American Anthropological Association.

Little, Kenneth
1963   The Context of Social Change. In The Teaching of Anthropology. D. G. Mandelbaum et. al. (eds.). Memoir 94, Washington, D. C.: American Anthropological Association.

Mandelbaum, David G.
1963   Introduction. In The Teaching of Anthropology. D. G. Mandelbaum et al (eds.). Memoir 94. Washington, D. C.: American Anthropological Association.

Paul, Benjamin D.
1963   Teaching Cultural Anthropology in Schools of Public Health. In The Teaching of Anthropology. D.G. Mandelbaum, et al (eds.). Memoir 94, Washington, D.C.: American Anthropological Association.

Rapoport, Robert N.
1963   Aims and Methods. In The Teaching of Anthropology. D. G.
        Mandelbaum et al (eds.). Memoir 94, Washington, D. C.:
        American Anthropological Association.

Thompson, Laura
1963   Concepts and Contributions. In The Teaching of Anthropology.
        D. G. Mandelbaum et al (eds.). Memoir 94, Washington, D.C.:
        American Anthropological Association.

202   UNITED STATES   1960

A research project in Applied Anthropology for the Jicarilla Apache
Tribe dealt with political and economic development on the Jicarilla
reservation. It was supported by the Tribal Government and was not
an action program.

Basehart, Harry W. and Tom T. Sasaki
1964   Changing Political Organization in the Jicarilla Apache
        Reservation Community, Human Organization, 23(4)283-289.

Wolfe, Leo J.
1961   The Relationship Between Unearned Income and Individual
        Productive Effort on the Jicarilla Apache Reservation,
        Economic Development and Cultural Change, 9(4):589-597.

203   INDIA   1960

Verrier Elwin headed an official government committee to review the
operations of the Special Multipurpose Tribal Blocks for the
Ministry of Home Affairs.

Elwin, Verrier
1960   Report of the Committee on Special Multipurpose Tribal
        Blocks. New Delhi: Ministry of Home Affairs.

204   UNITED STATES   1961

American Indian Chicago Conference was organized,..."as a test of
action anthropology in response to Indian dissatisfaction with
federal policy of the 1950's." (Lurie, 1976) The conference,
which was coordinated by Sol Tax, stimulated the development of the
National Indian Youth Council, the Great Lakes Inter-Tribal Council,
as well as political organization of the Winnebago of Wisconsin
under the provisions of the Indian Reorganization Act.

American Indian Chicago Conference
1961   Declaration of Indian Purpose: The Voice of the American
        Indian, Chicago: American Indian Chicago Conference.

Lurie, Nancy O.
1976   Comment. Human Organization, 35(3)320-321.

BIBLIOGRAPHIC CHRONOLOGY 205-208

205 UNITED STATES 1961

John F. Kennedy appointed Philleo Nash and James E. Officer to a task force to examine federal Indian Policy. Their general orientation was toward increasing self-determination in American Indian communities

Spicer, Edward H.
1977   Early Applications of Anthropology in North America. In Perspectives on Anthropology, 1976. Anthony F. C. Wallace et al (eds.). Washington, D. C.: American Anthropological Association (a special publication of the American Anthropological Association Number 10).

206 INDIA 1961

The Census of India retained anthropologists to do a special series of village studies. These studies resulted in good quality data on microdevelopment.

Adelman, Irma and George Dalton
1971   A Factor Analysis of Modernization in Village India. In Economic Development and Social Change. George Dalton (ed.). New York: Natural History Press.

Mathur, H. M.
1976   Anthropology, Government and Development Planning in India. In Development from Below, Anthropologists and Development Situations. David C. Pitt. (ed.). The Hague: Mouton Publishers.

207 UNITED STATES 1961

After an earlier political career as administrative assistant to President Harry S Truman and Lieutenant Governor of Wisconsin, Philleo Nash was nominated by President Kennedy as U. S. Commissioner of Indian Affairs. This was not done without difficulty as Nash explains, "I have to say to other applied anthropologists that I was confirmed in spite of being an anthropologist, not because of it. The Senate of the United States in those days did not think it wise to have a believer in the worth of indigenous cultures serving as Commissioner of Indian Affairs (1979:23)".

Nash, Philleo
1979   Anthropologist in the White House. Practicing Anthropologist. 1(3):3,23,24.

208 UNITED STATES 1961

The establishment of the Peace Corps resulted in the placement of anthropologists as administrators, policy-makers, evaluators, trainers, and volunteers.

Comitas, Lambros
1966   Lessons from Jamaica. In Cultural Frontiers of the Peace Corps. Robert B. Textor, (ed.). Cambridge: MIT.

Dorjahn, Vernon R.
1966   Transcultural Perceptions and Mispreceptions in Sierra Leone. In Cultural Frontiers of the Peace Corps. Robert Textor, (ed.). Cambridge: MIT.

Doughty, Paul
1966   Pitfalls and Progress in the Peruvian Sierra. In Cultural Frontiers of the Peace Corps. Robert B. Textor, (ed.). Cambridge: MIT.

Dupree, Louis
1966   Moving Mountains in Afghanistan. In Cultural Frontiers of the Peace Corps. Robert B. Textor, (ed.). Cambridge: MIT.

Heath, Dwight B.
1966   The Emerging Volunteer Subculture in Bolivia. In Cultural Frontiers of the Peace Corps. Robert B. Textor, (ed.). Cambridge: MIT.

Mahony, Frank J.
1961   Evaluation of a Pilot Project in Range Management near Afmadu. Community Development Review. 6(1).

1966   Success in Somalia. In Cultural Frontiers of the Peace Corps. Robert B. Textor, (ed.). Cambridge: MIT.

Maretzki, Thomas
1965   Transition Training: A Theoretical Approach. Human Organization, 24(2):128-134.

Patch, Richard W.
1964   Vicos and the Peace Corps: A Failure in Intercultural Communication, American Universities Field Staff Reports, 11(2).

Szanton, David L.
1966   Cultural Confrontation in the Philippines. In Cultural Frontiers of the Peace Corps. Robert B. Textor, (ed.). Cambridge: MIT.

Textor, Robert B., (ed.)
1966   Cultural Frontiers of the Peace Corps. Cambridge: MIT.

ETHIOPIA   1962

Working under the auspices of the United States Agency for International Development, Simon D. Messing served in a public health demonstration and evaluation team which conducted research in rural Ethiopia. The team dealt with various groups including the Amhara, Galla, Tigre,

Somali, Kambatta, Wollamo, Anauk and Nuer. The team's primary goal
was to measure the effects of new health care centers.

Messing, Simon D.
1965   Application of Health Questionnaires to Pre-Urban
Communities in a Developing Country. Human Organization.
24(3).

1964   "Base-Line Health Culture Research in a Developing Country,
Public Health Research in Ethiopia for USAID." American
Behavioral Scientist. 7(8).

210   UNITED STATES   1962

George Foster's Traditional Cultures and the Impact of Technical
Change was published.

Foster, George M.
1962   Traditional Cultures and The Impact of Technical Change.
New York: Harper and Row.

211   GHANA   1962

The Volta River Project, initiated by Kwame Nkrumah Prime Minister
of Ghana, resulted in the construction of a major hydro-electric
dam and the displacement of 67,000 people. The project made limited
use of anthropological data in the planning stages.

Brokensha, David
1963   Volta Resettlement and Anthropological Research. Human
Organization. 22(4):286-290.

212   UNITED STATES   1962

Studies of American Indian educational systems (particularly among
the Sioux) by Murray L. Wax and Rosalie Wax encouraged the development of more encompassing American Indian educational studies by
causing uneasiness in relevant educational circles. The Wax's
work gave impetus to the idea of Indian control of schools.

Wax, Murray L., Rosalie H. Wax and R. V. Dumont, Jr.
1964   Formal Education in an Indian Community. Monograph No. 1,
Society for the Study of Social Problems.

213   UNITED STATES   1962

According to Steven Polgar, Moni Nag's Factors Affecting Human
Fertility in Non-Industrial Societies: A Cross-cultural Study, led
to the recognition of population anthropology as a significant
subspecialty.

Nag, Moni
1962   Factors Affecting Human Fertility in Non-industrial
        Societies: A Cross Cultural Study. Yale University
        Publications in Anthropology, No. 66.

214   VENEZUELA   1962

The Joint Center for Urban Studies Guyana Project employed
anthropologist Lisa R. Peattie to work with an interdisciplinary
team planning a new city in the interior of Venezuela.

Peattie, Lisa R.
1968   The View from the Barrio. Ann Arbor: University of
            Michigan Press.

1969a   Conflicting Views of the Project: Caracas Versus the
            Site. In Regional Planning for Development: The
            Experience of the Guayani Program of Venezuela. Lloyd
            Rodwin (ed.). Cambridge, Mass: M.I.T. Press.

1969b   Social Mobility and Economic Development. In Regional
            Planning for Development: The Experience of the Guayani
            Program of Venezuela. Lloyd Rodwin (ed.). Cambridge,
            Mass: M.I.T. Press

215   UNITED STATES   1963

An early example of the benefits of including behavioral science
faculty in medical schools is an evaluation study carried out by
anthropologist Marion Pearsall in collaboration with the Department
of Nursing of the University of Kentucky. The anthropologist nurse
collaboration led to an effective refocus of nursing services.

Pearsall, Marion and M. Sue Kern
1967   Behavioral Science, Nursing Services, and the Collaborative
            Process: A Case Study. Journal of Applied Behavioral
            science, 3(2):243-270.

216   UNITED STATES   1963

Steven Polgar was hired as Director of Research at the Planned
Parenthood Federation of America.

Polgar, Steven
1977   Anthropologists and Birth Planning-1935 to 1975.
            unpublished paper.

217   VIET-NAM   1963

Anthropologist Howard K. Kaufman who was employed by A.I.D. was
temporarily assigned the duty of evaluating the success of a Viet-
Namese fishing cooperative in Khanh Hou Province. During this time
Kaufman was employed by Commissioner General of Cooperatives of the

Republic of Vietnam.

Kaufman, Howard K.
1974   Culao-A Vietnamese Fishing Cooperative and Its Problems in Social Organization and the Applications of Anthropology, Essays in Honor of Lauriston Sharp. Robert J. Smith (ed.). Ithaca: Cornell University Press.

218 UNITED STATES   1963

Cooperation in Change, by Ward H. Goodenough, which is a useful compilation of theory concerning the application of cultural theory to problems of development and technical assistance was published. It was one of three manuals for administrators stimulated by the Cornell Summer Field School in Applied Anthropology in the early 1950's.

Goodenough, Ward H.
1963   Cooperation in Change. Anthropological Approaches to Community Development. New York: Russell Sage Foundation.

219 UNITED STATES   1963

A anthropologist-physician team initiated a program which was designed to eradicate tuberculosis in Martin County, Kentucky. The strategy involved coordination of health care agencies from within and from outside the community; combination of both social science and medical expertise, integration of both clinical and public health approaches, and the use of action research techniques.

Hochstrasser, Donald L.
1966   Community Health Work in Southern Appalachia, Mountain Life and Work, 42(3):7-16.

1966   It's All-Out-War on TB in an Appalachian County. Bulletin, National Tuberculosis Association, 52(1):3-8.

Hochstrasser, Donald L., G. S. Nickerson and Kurt W. Deuschle
1966   Sociomedical Approaches to Community Health Programs. Milbank Memorial Fund Quarterly, 44(3):345-359.

220 UNITED STATES   1964

Project Camelot was a multidisciplinary project designed to produce improved understanding of the causes of civil war in Latin America. Sponsored by the United States Department of Defense, the project led to a significant ethical debate in anthropology.

Horowitz, Irving Louis, ed.
1974   The Rise and Fall of Project Camelot, Studies in the Relationship Between Social Science and Practical Politics. Cambridge: M.I.T.

Nisbet, Robert A.
1974   Project Camelot and the Science of Man. In The Rise and
        Fall of Project Camelot. L. Horowitz, (ed.). Cambridge:
        M.I.T.

221   UNITED STATES   1964

The U. S. Office of Education funded a project entitled, "Development of a Sequential Curriculum in Anthropology for Grades 1-7" to be carried out at the University of Georgia. The project involved Wilfrid C. Bailey and Francis J. Clune, Jr. as well as various consultants.

Bailey, Wilfrid C.
1966   Anthropology Curriculum Project, University of Georgia.
        Fellow Newsletter. 7(7):9-10.

222   BRITISH SOLOMONS   1964

The Wagina Resettlement Scheme in the Western Pacific had anthropologists as administrators.

Cochrane, Glyn
1970   The Administration of Wagina Resettlement Scheme.
        Human Organization. 29(2):123-132.

223   UNITED STATES   1964

Establishment of the McKinley County, New Mexico, Community Treatment Plan for Navaho Problem Drinkers. The project made use of anthropologists and illustrated the increasing use of anthropologically trained persons in clinical settings.

Ferguson, Frances Northend
1968   Navaho Drinking: Some Tentative Hypotheses. Human
        Organization. 27(2):159-167.

224   UNITED STATES   1964

Murray L. Wax and Rosalie H. Wax studied "drop-outs" among American Indian students for the United States Office of Education. Materials derived from the research were presented before the Special Subcommittee on Indian Education of the Committee on Labor and Public Welfare.

Wax, Murray L. and Rosalie H. Wax
1969   Dropout of American Indians at the Secondary Level.
        Hearings before the Special Subcommittee on Indian
        Education of the Committee on Labor and Public Welfare.
        U. S. Senate 90th Congress, Part 4, pp. 1457-1523,
        Washington, D. C.: Government Printing Office.

225 UNITED STATES 1965

   The Center for Developmental Change at the University of Kentucky
   contracted with the Office of Economic Opportunity to evaluate
   Community Action Programs in rural Kentucky. The multidisciplinary
   team included anthropologists Art Gallaher, Jr. and Stephen R. Cain.

   Cain, Stephen R.
   1968   A Selective Description of a Knox County Mountain Neigh-
           borhood Unit 3. In An Appraisal of the "War on Poverty"
           in a Rural Setting of Southeastern Kentucky. (Photocopy)

226 UNITED STATES 1965

   The first Nurse-Anthropologists were graduated. These individuals
   were the products of federally sponsored programs which provided
   training in anthropology to registered nurses. In 1969, the
   Society for Medical Anthropology organized its Committee on Nursing
   and Anthropology. Madeline Leininger served as the initial chairman.

   Leininger, Madeline M.
   1967   The Culture Concept and its Relevance to Nursing. The
           Journal of Nursing Education. 6(2):27-39.

   1968   The Significance of Cultural Concepts in Nursing.
           Minnesota League for Nursing Bulletin. 16(3):3-12.

   1968   The Use of Cultural Concepts in Patient Care. Minnesota
           League for Nursing Bulletin, 16(5):3-4.

   1970   Nursing and Anthropology: Two Worlds to Blend. John
           Wiley: New York.

227 NIGERIA 1966

   The International Institute of Tropical Agriculture developed an
   agricultural resettlement project to increase agricultural production.
   Anthropologically trained personnel were included as researchers
   and planners.

   Smock, David R.
   1969   The Role of Anthropology in a Western Nigerian Resettlement
           Project. In The Anthropology of Development in Sub-Saharan
           Africa. David Brokensha and Marion Pearsall, (eds.).
           Society for Applied Anthropology, Monograph No. 10.

228 UNITED STATES 1965

   The Peace Corps Act of 1961 was amended at the suggestion of Sergeant
   Shriver. The change specified that above the grade of GS-9 no person
   could be employed by the Peace Corps for more than five years. This
   provided legal sanction for the so-called In-Up-Out policy developed
   by Robert B. Textor. This policy controlled staffing of Peace Corps
   Washington offices to returned volunteers who worked for a limited
   amount of time.

Textor, Robert B.
1966   Conclusions, Problems and Prospects. In Cultural Frontiers of the Peace Corps. R. B. Textor (ed.). Cambridge, MA: M.I.T. Press.

229 ZAMBIA   1966

The Kariba Dam Project led to major population displacement. To a limited extent, anthropologists were involved in basic documentation and policy-research on this attempt to increase agricultural output in the Zambezi basin.

Scudder, Thayer
1965   The Kariba Case: Man-Made Lakes and Resource Development in Africa, Bulletin of the Atomic Scientist, 21:6-11.

1968   Social Anthropology, Man-Made Lakes and Population Relocation in Africa, Anthropological Quarterly, 41.

1969   Relocation, Agricultural Intensification, and Anthropological Research. In the Anthropology of Development in Sub-Saharan Africa. David Brokensha and Marion Pearsall, (eds.). Society for Applied Anthropology, Monograph No. 10.

230 UNITED STATES   1966

Urban Planning Aid, an advocacy planning group in Boston, was created to serve an advocacy function in planning for certain low-income Boston neighborhoods. The organization made use of anthropologists in advocacy planning roles.

Peattie, Lisa R.
1968   Reflections on Advocacy Planning. American Institute of Planners. 34:80-87.

231 UNITED STATES   1966

Edward H. Spicer and William Willard were employed in community development administration in a Southwestern Indian community.

Spicer, Edward H.
1970   Patrons of the Poor, Human Organization. 29(1):12-19.

Willard, William
1977   The Agency Camp Project, Human Organization, 36(4):352-362.

232 UNITED STATES   1967

What was later to be called the Society for Medical Anthropology held its first formal organizational meeting at the American Anthropological Association meetings in Washington. The steering committee created consisted of Clifford R. Barnett, Donald A. Kennedy, Benjamin D. Paul,

Marion Pearsall, Steven Polgar, Norman A. Scotch, Ailoh Shiloh,
Hazel H. Werdman and Paul E. White.

1968 Medical Anthropologists Meet. Fellow Newsletter.
9(2):3

233 UNITED STATES 1967

Various anthropologists have been hired to evaluate component programs of the Office of Economic Opportunity. In one such case John L. Sorenson and Larry L. Berg evaluated the Indian Community Action Programs at Arizona State University, University of South Dakota and the University of Utah. The evaluation design involved extensive interviewing. The Indian Community Action Programs were depicted as sensitive to the needs of Indian communities.

Sorenson, John L. and Larry L. Berg
1967 Evaluation of Indian Community Action Programs at Arizona State University, University of South Dakota and University of Utah (CR-82-1). General Research Corporation, Santa Barbara, California.

234 KENYA

The use of anthropologists by the World Bank has been quite limited. According to Husain the earliest use seems to have been in the evaluation of livestock development projects in Kenya. The Bank hired N. Dyson-Hudson to evaluate a project which was to improve rangeland utilization in Kenya and to transform traditional pastoralists to greater market participation. The project involved the establishment of "group ranches" for Masai families and certain programatic design features calculated to avoid overgrazing. Basic elements of design were suggested by the anthropologist. Dyson-Hudson carried out similar work in Kenya in 1972.

Husain, Tariq
1976 Use of Anthropologists in Project Appraisal by the World Bank. In Development from Below, Anthropologists and Development Situations. David C. Pitt (ed.) the Hague: Mouton Publishers.

235 UNITED STATES 1967

The Society for American Archaeology created the Committee on the Public Understanding of Archaeology which was later renamed Committee on Public Archeology. At the present time COPA functions as a communication network on archeologically-relevant political issues, such as federal agency review deadlines.

Committee on Public Archeology, Society for American Archaeology.
1979   What is COPA? COPA Communication, (January) p.1.

236   UNITED STATES   1967

In a relationship which evolved out of a dissertation project John H. Peterson, Jr. became chief planner for the Mississippi Band of Choctaws. In this role he participated in an array of development projects as a researcher. This included employment and housing development.

Peterson, John H., Jr.
1970   Socio-Economic Characteristics of the Mississippi Choctaw Indians. Social Science Research Center Report No. 34. State College: Mississippi State University.

1972   Assimilation, Separation and Out-Migration in an American Indian Community. American Anthropologist. 74:1286-1295.

1974   The Anthropologist as Advocate. Human Organization. 33:311-318.

1978   The Changing Role of an Applied Anthropologist. In Applied Anthropology in America. Elizabeth M. Eddy and William L. Partridge (eds.).· Columbia University Press: New York.

237   CANADA   1967

Assisted by Anthropologist Walter Hlady, Cree and Meti fur trappers in the Saskatchewan River Delta area attempted to develop an alternative to the Hudson's Bay Company. Hlady was employed by the Citizenship Branch of the Canadian Department of State and given free rein to assist the community. Hudson's Bay Company held the fur trading lease in the area, but wanted to be relieved of the responsibility and thereby requested that the Province reassign the lease prior to its expiration and buy out the company's equity. Hlady's role was to provide the community with information on the various alternatives and support the community in its dealings with the Provincial government.

Lurie, Nancy O.
1973   Action Anthropology and the American Indian. Anthropology and the American Indian, Report of a Symposium. San Francisco: Indian Historian Press.

Hlady, Walter M.
1969   The Cumberland House Fur Project: The First Two Years. Western Canadian Journal of Anthropology. 1(1).

238 UNITED STATES   1967

　　　　Project Headstart, which became a very important component of the
　　　　"War on Poverty," made use of anthropologists in limited numbers
　　　　as evaluators. One example of these activities was the work of
　　　　the Bank Street College of Education, Research Division in a number
　　　　of New Jersey schools between 1967 and 1973.

　　　　Jacobsen, Claire
　　　　1973   The Organization of Work in a Pre-school Setting:
　　　　 Work Relations Between Professionals and Paraprofessionals
　　　　 in Four Head Start Centers, New York: Bank Street College
　　　　 of Education (available through ERIC).

239 UNITED STATES   1968

　　　　The Mexican American Education Project is a research and development
　　　　project initiated at California State University, Sacramento. Its
　　　　initial funding came from the U. S. Office of Education. The
　　　　general mission of the project was the improvement of educational
　　　　opportunities for Mexican-Americans. Early leadership for the
　　　　project came from Warren Snyder who was Chairman of the Anthropology
　　　　Department at California State University, Sacramento and Steven
　　　　F. Arvizu.

　　　　Specific programs were developed in the following areas: fellowship
　　　　program for experienced teachers, curriculum development, fellowships
　　　　for "high risk, high gain" individuals, prospective teachers and
　　　　an early childhood component.

　　　　Arvizu, Steven F.
　　　　1973   The Mexican American Education Project Final Report.
　　　　 California State University, Sacramento.

240 UNITED STATES   1968

　　　　Using an approach which is termed by Rios as action anthropology,
　　　　California State University at Sacramento, anthropologist Senon
　　　　Valadez developed a program of community oriented courses for
　　　　Chicanos in Sacramento. These activities were designed to bridge
　　　　the gap between the university and the community. One of these
　　　　was the Chicanito Science Project which was to attract young Chicanos
　　　　to science. From this base, action anthropology activities extended
　　　　to other courses as well as to nutrition programs and art programs.

　　　　Rios, Sam
　　　　1978   An Approach to Action Anthropology: The Community
　　　　 Project, C.S.U.S. In Grito del Sol, a Chicano Quarterly
　　　　 (Year three-Book one, January-March 1978). Steven F.
　　　　 Arvizu (ed.).

241-243 ANTHROPOLOGY IN USE

241   UNITED STATES   1968

Using ethnosemantic research techniques, James Spradley investigated aspects of the life of the Seattle urban alcoholic. This project contributed to certain reforms in the Seattle legal system. These reforms included the decriminalization of public drunkenness and the establishment of a detoxification center for alcoholics.

Spradley, James P.
1970   You Owe Yourself a Drunk, An Ethnography of Urban Nomads. Boston: Little, Brown.

1970   Adaptive Strategies of Urban Nomads: The Ethnoscience of Tramp Culture. In The Anthropology of Urban Environments. Weaver and White, (eds.). Society for Applied Anthropology.

242   UNITED STATES   1968

The National Study of Indian Education was begun to review, in global terms, the state of the education system which served American Indian communities. The massive project benefited by the participation of a substantial number of anthropologists. These included John Chilcott, Bryan Michener, John Collier, Jr., Margaret Knight, and John H. Peterson, Jr. Over 40 schools were studied.

Aurbach, Herbert A. and Estelle Fuchs
1970   The Status of American Indian Education. Interim report of NSAIE. Pennsylvania State University.

Fuchs, Estelle and Robert J. Havighurst
1970   To Live on this Earth: American Indian Education. New York: Doubleday.

243   UNITED STATES   1968

The Papago Tribe of Arizona hired anthropologists in various administrative positions. These people included John van Willigen who was the Director of Community Development for the Tribe and Barry R. Bainton who was Legal Education Officer.

van Willigen, John
1971   The Papago Community Development Worker. Community Development Journal. 6(2).

1973   Abstract Goals and Concrete Means: Papago Experiences in the Application of Development Resources. Human Organization, 32(1).

1976   Applied Anthropology and Community Development: A Critical Assessment. In Do Applied Anthropologists Apply Anthropology?. M. Angrosino (ed.). Proceedings of the Southern Anthropological Society, University of Georgia Press.

1977   Administrative Problems in an Arizona Community Development Programme. Community Development Journal. 12(1).

244 UNITED STATES — 1968

"Action Research," or "Community Advocacy" anthropology approaches were developed on the Southside of Chicago. An anthropologist served as a researcher in association with the indigenous leadership of the community to assist achieving community goals. The approach is conceptually related to both research and development and action anthropology.

Schensul, Stephen L.
1973   Action Research: The Applied Anthropologist in a Community Mental Health Program. In Anthropology Beyond the University. A. Redfield, (ed.), Southern Anthropological Society Proceedings No. 7. Athens: University of Georgia Press.

1974   Skills Needed in Action Anthropology: Lessons from El Centro de la Causa. Human Organization, 33:203-209.

245 UNITED STATES — 1968

Various anthropologists developed serious interest in research into the cultural dimensions of drug use. In some cases this interest developed into anthropologists acting as therapists. These therapies were based on strategies of reenculturation.

Rosenstiel, C. R. and J. B. Freeland
1973   Anthropological Perspectives on the Rehabilitation of Institutionalized Narcotic Addicts. In Anthropology Beyond the University, Proceedings of the Southern Anthropological Society, No. 6, Alden Redfield, (ed.) Athens University of Georgia Press.

Weppner, Robert S.
1973   An Anthropological View of the Street Addict's World. Human Organization. 32(2):111-112.

246 UNITED STATES — 1969

Public Television-Radio in Tucson, Arizona KUAT-TV-AM/FM developed Project Fiesta which was calculated to attract, entertain and inform Mexican-Americans. The project used anthropological research techniques in program planning and development and in the ultimate evaluation. The project was funded by the Ford Foundation. The research coordinator of the project was anthropologist E. B. Eiselein.

Eiselein, E. B. and Wes Marshall
1976   Mexican-American Television: Applied Anthropology and Public Television. Human Organization. 35(2):147-156.

Eiselein, E. B. and Wes Marshall
1971   Fiesta--An Experiment in Minority Audience Research and Programming. Educational Television, 3(2):11-15.

Marshall, Wes, E. B. Eiselein, J. T. Duncan and R. Gomez
1974   Fiesta: Minority Television Programming. Tucson: University of Arizona Press.

247 UNITED STATES — 1969

Anthropologist Fay G. Cohen developed a thesis research project which focused on a component of the program of the Minneapolis based American Indian Movement. Working closely with Dennis Banks and Clyde Bellecourt, Cohen was able to assist AIM in a number of areas. She did some basic writing and documentation for AIM and ultimately became a member. Her access to information became a reciprocal of the services she offered to AIM.

Cohen, Fay G.
1973a   The Indian Patrol in Minneapolis: Social Control and Social Change in an Urban Context. Unpublished Ph.D. dissertation, University of Minnesota.

1973b   The Indian Patrol in Minneapolis: Social Control and Social Change in an Urban Context. Law and Society Review. 7:779-786.

1976   The American Indian Movement and the Anthropologist: Issues and Implications of Consent. In Dilemmas in Fieldwork, Ethics and Anthropology. Michael A. Rynkiewich and James P. Spradley (eds.). New York: John Wiley.

248 UNITED STATES — 1969

The National Environmental Policy Act (P.L. 91-190) was passed, obligating federal agencies to prepare an environmental impact statement for every major federal action which affects the human environment. This included both the cultural and physical environments and consequently constitutes the most important legislation offering protection to archaeological resources. The Archeological and Historic Preservation Act of 1974 (P.L. 93-291) extended this protection to all remains which might be lost as a result of federal construction or other federally licensed or aided activities, and provided that up to one percent of the project funds could be used for this purpose. The full impact of new employment opportunities and changing paradigms for research initiated under these acts has yet to be fully assessed, but are already fostering drastic changes in the discipline.

Lipe, W. D. and A. J. Lindsay, Jr. (eds.)
1974   Proceedings of the 1974 Cultural Resource Management Conference. Flagstaff, AR: Museum of Northern Arizona (Technical Series 14).

McGimsey, Charles R., III
1972   Public Archeology. New York: Seminar Press.

249   THAILAND   1970

Student Mobilization Committee to End the War in Vietnam representatives stole papers from an UCLA anthropologist which were used to mount an attack on the involvement of anthropologists and other social scientists in Thailand research during the Vietnam War. The documents were perceived as indicating that anthropologists were involved in secret research funded by the Agency for International Development which focused upon "accelerating rural development" and village security. These perceptions resulted in an extensive debate within the American Anthropological Association. The case was investigated by the Association's Committee on Ethics.

Belshaw, Cyril S.
1976   The Sorcerer's Apprentice, An Anthropology of Public Policy. New York: Pergamon Press.

Wolf, Eric and Joseph Jorgensen
1970   Anthropology on the Warpath in Thailand, New York Review of Books. 15(9): November 19).

250   UNITED STATES   1970

The Hopi Tribe of Arizona initiated a Headstart "Follow Through Program" in 1968. This program was studied by Murray L. Wax and Robert G. Breunig who focused upon identifying how Hopi parents defined formal education. Wax and Breunig concluded that Hopis viewed schools as white institutions and that this conception did not change as a result of parental involvement programs.

Wax, Murray L. and Robert G. Breunig
1973   Study of the Community Impact of the Hopi Follow Through Program. (Final Report, Project No. 2-0647, Grant No. OEG-0-72-3946). U. S. Department of Health, Education and Welfare, Office of Education, National Institute of Education.

251   CANADA   1970

Project Canada West represented a major attempt to develop school curriculum appropriate to the needs of the ethnically diverse western portion of Canada. The project made substantial use of anthropology. Participating anthropologists provided information to curriculum development specialists on various ethnic groups.

Sabey, Ralph H.
1973   The Preparation of Culturally Sensitive Curriculum Material for Canadian Schools: An Overview. Council on Anthropology and Education Newsletter. 4(2):7-10.

252–254 ANTHROPOLOGY IN USE

252   UNITED STATES   1970

Under contract with the Public Health Service, research was conducted on the Papago Reservation to measure the impact of improved housing program of the Department of Housing and Urban Development on health and work productivity, and evaluate the architectural and proxemic design of housing preferred by the Papago. Anthropologist Robert M. Wulff was site director with a project team that included public health personnel and Papago interviewers and translators.

Wulff, Robert M.
1972   Housing the Papago: An Analytical Critique of a Housing Delivery System. International Housing Productivity Report University of California, Los Angeles.

1973   Papago Architecture and Modernization: Style and Proxemic Preferences, Southwestern Anthropology Association Newsletter (October)

253   UNITED STATES   1970

Glyn Cochrane initiated a working relationship with the World Bank so as to demonstrate the utility of anthropology in international development. Cochrane did a study of World Bank operations to determine where anthropology might be useful.

Cochrane, Glyn
1976   The Perils of Unconventional Anthropology. In Development from Below, Anthropologists and Development Situations. David C. Pitt (ed.) the Hague: Mouton Publishers.

254   BRAZIL   1970

Using concepts derived from anthropology, Paulo Freire developed what he referred to as the <u>conscientizacion</u> method of inducing change. He attempted to diffuse technical skills to illiterate and passive peasants in northeastern Brazil and Chile. As part of these efforts he worked to increase the peasants' capacity for critical judgements. Freire focused upon the concept of culture, as he notes," Culture, as an interiorized product which in turn conditions men's subsequent acts, must become the object of men's knowledge so that they can perceive its conditioning power" (1970: 16).

Freire, Paulo
1970   Cultural Action for Freedom. Harvard Educational Review and Center for the Study of Development and Social Change. Monograph Series No. 1.

1972   Pedagogy of the Oppressed. New York: Herder and Herder.

1973   Education for Critical Consciousness. New York: The Seabury Press.

255 UNITED STATES 1970

Lisa R. Peattie was employed by the Boston Housing Authority as a researcher.

Peattie, Lisa R.
1971a   Public Housing: Urban Slums under Public Management. In Race, Change and Urban Society, Urban Affairs Annual Review. P. Orleans and W. Ellis (eds.) Sage Publications.

1971b   Conventional Public Housing. Working Paper No. 3. Joint Center for Urban Studies.

256 PERU 1971

The International Potato Center (CIP) was established to increase the yield of potatoes in the developing countries. Located in Lima, CIP maintains research and training programs in the agronomic and social sciences. Anthropologists have been employed as participants in the social science component which does both research and training. Research includes both literature review and field work. Research efforts focus on the entire potato using process from growing to storage and processing.

Werge, Robert W.
1977   Anthropology and Agricultural Research: The Case of Potato Anthropology. CIP Socioeconomic Unit. Lima: Centro Internacional de la Papa.

257 UNITED STATES 1971

A Rockefeller Foundation funded research project was initiated in order to provide research results to the Oregon State government and legislature. Entitled, "Man's Activities as Related to Environmental Quality." One of the projects carried out under the aegis of this grant was done by anthropologist John A. Young who investigated the motivations and adaptations of In-migrants to the Willamette Valley. The investigation was done with a small sample (N=37) using a series of focused interviews. These interview data were subjected to a factor analysis which allowed the classification of the respondents in various categories, e.g. restless Californian, Drifters, Working Class, Mavericks, etc.

Young, John A.
1975   Migrants in Three Willamette Valley Towns: Why They Move and How They Adapt. Prepared for the Rockefeller Foundation Project "Man's Activities as Related to Environmental Quality" Corvallis: Oregon State University.

258   UNITED STATES   1971

As part of their struggle to maintain the appropriateness of their education system, the Old Order Amish of Wisconsin resisted public school consolidation and compulsory secondary education. As part of their resistance efforts the Amish benefited from data supplied by anthropologist John Hostetler. Hostetler had carried out a basic research project focused on Old Order Amish socialization and education. He testified before the Supreme Court.

Hostetler, John A.
1972   Amish Schooling: A Study in Alternatives. Council on Anthropology and Education Newsletter. 3(2):1-4.

Hostetler, John A. and G. E. Huntington
1971   Children in Amish Society: Socialization and Community Education. New York: Holt, Rinehart and Winston.

259   UNITED STATES   1971

The Health Ecology Project was developed in Miami, Florida, to incorporate anthropological theory and knowledge into "The training of health professionals, the structure of the health care system, and the delivery of health care." (Weidman, 1976: 106) A key concept in the project is that of culture broker. The culture broker is a collaborating professional member of the health-care delivery team who serves as link and mediator between a cultural group and the health care providers.

Bryant, Carol A.
1975   The Puerto Rican Mental Health Unit. Psychiatric Annals. 5(8):333-338.

Carroo, Agatha E.
1975   A Black Community in Limbo. Psychiatric Annals. 5(8):320-323.

Lefley, Harriet P.
1975   Approaches to Community Mental Health: The Miami Model. Psychiatric Annals. 5(9):315-319.

Sandoval, Mercedes C. and Leon Tozo
1975   An Emergent Cuban Community. Psychiatric Annals. 5(9):324-332.

Weidman, Hazel H.
1971   Trained Manpower and Medical Anthropology: Conceptual, Organizational and Educational Priorities. Social Science and Medicine. 5(1):15-36.

1973   Implications of the Culture-Broker Concept for the Delivery of Health Care. Paper presented at the meetings of the Southern Anthropological Society, Wrightsville Beach, North Carolina.

1974   Toward the Goal of Responsiveness in Mental Health Care. Paper presented at Department of Psychiatry, University of Miami.

1975   Concepts as Strategies for Change. A Psychiatric Annals Reprint. New York: Insight Communications.

1976   In Praise of the Double Bind Inherent in Anthropological Application. In Do Applied Anthropologists Apply Anthropology? M. Angrosino (ed.) Proceedings of the Southern Anthropological Society, No. 10. Athens: University of Georgia Press.

Wiedman, Hazel H. and Janice A. Egeland
1973   A Behavioral Science Perspective in the Comparative Approach to the Delivery of Health Care, Social Science and Medicine. 7(11):845-860.

260   UNITED STATES   1971

University Year for Action, as it was implemented at the University of Wisconsin-Green Bay, used applied anthropology techniques and concepts. The program, which was both service providing and instructional, dealt with nine Native American communities in Northern Wisconsin. The project included grant-seeking and lobbying activities.

Hunter, David E. and Phillip Whitten
1976   Fieldwork II: Applied Anthropology Among Wisconsin's Native Americans. In The Study of Anthropology. New York: Harper and Row.

261   UNITED STATES   1971

Karl Schlesier, an anthropologist and ethnohistorian contacted representatives of the Southern Cheyenne in 1968 to carry out basic historical research. From this emerged a working relationship defined by Schlesier as action anthropology. Working closely with the Arrowkeeper, a traditional and sacred Southern Cheyenne leadership role, Schlesier attempted to foster and encourage the reemergence of significant traditional leadership. This was expressed both through traditional roles and a group named the Southern Cheyenne Research and Human Development Association.

Schlesier, Karl H.
1974   Action Anthropology and the Southern Cheyenne. Current Anthropology. 15(3):277-283.

262-264 ANTHROPOLOGY IN USE

262 UNITED STATES   1971

Anthropologists participated in a multi-disciplinary research team which evaluated the potential for industrial development in a rural region of Arkansas. Government policy makers expressed concern that the local labor force manifested characteristics which would preclude effective industrial development. The Grinstead study revealed a high potential for success for potential workers. Her study made use of such concepts as "job satisfaction potential" and "internal-external control."

Davis, R. N., B. L. Green and J. M. Redfern
1975   Low-Income Rural People in East Central Arkansas Face Roadblocks to Jobs. Washington, D. C.: Agricultural Economic Report No. 290.

Grinstead, M. J.
1976   Poverty, Race and Culture in a Rural Arkansas Community, Human Organization. 35(1):33-34.

Grinstead, M. J., B. L. Green and J. M. Redfern
1974   Social and Labor Adjustment of Rural Black Americans in the Mississippi Delta: A Case Study of Madison, Ark.. Washington, D. C.: Agricultural Economic Report, No. 274.

1975   Rural Development and Labor Adjustment in the Mississippi Delta and Ozarks of Arkansas: A Summary Report. Fayetteville, AR: Agricultural Experiment Station Bulletin 795.

263 NEW GUINEA   1971

A dispute developed between two factions of the politically sophisticated Tolai language group. The two groups were divided in terms of "nationalist" and "separatist" orientations. Richard Salisbury was retained as a consultant to attempt to solve the problem.

Salisbury, Richard F.
1969   Vunamam. Berkeley: University of California Press.

1971   Problems of the Gazelle Pennisula of New Britain, August 1971, Port Moresby: Government Printer.

1976   The Anthropologist as Societal Omsbudsman. In Development from Below, Anthropologists and Development Situations. David C. Pitt (ed.) the Hague: Mouton Publishers.

264 CANADA   1971

The Manitoba Metis Federation engaged an anthropologist to evaluate their housing needs. J. N. Kerri evaluated the housing development efforts of the Remote Housing Project, in particular. The RHP, as it was called, was to provide houses and create jobs. The field work and survey covered 48 communities.

Kerri, James N.
1977   A Social Analysis of the Human Element in Housing:
          A Canadian Case. Human Organization. 36(2):173-185.

265   UNITED STATES   1971

Frederick Gearing, anthropologist at State University of New York-Buffalo developed a training program in ethnographic observation for teachers, principals and supervisors from secondary schools. This project was carried out under contract to the Office of Education.

Gearing, Frederick O. and B. Allan Tindall
1973   Anthropological Studies of the Educational Process.
          Annual Review of Anthropology. Vol. 2, B. Siegel (ed.)
          Stanford, CA: Annual Reviews.

Gearing, Frederick, Wayne Hughes with Thomas Carroll, Walter Precourt and Allen Smith
1975   On Observing Well: Self Instruction in Ethnographic
          Observation for Teachers, Principals, and Supervisors.
          Amherst, N. Y.: Center for Studies of Cultural
          Transmission, SUNY-Buffalo.

266   UNITED STATES   1971

The Gila River Indian Community consisting largely of Pima and Maricopa Indians engaged a research team from the Bureau of Ethnic Research to evaluate and make recommendations to improve operations in the government of the community. Anthropologists involved included Thomas Weaver, project director and B. Alan Kite as co-investigator.

Weaver, Thomas et al
1971   Political Organization and Business Management in the
          Gila River Indian Community. (Research Report Series,
          June, 1971) Tucson: Bureau of Ethnic Research,
          University of Arizona.

267   TANZANIA   1972

Priscilla Reining, an American anthropologist, was retained by the World Bank to do a "Project Appraisal" of a program to organize pastoral people into so-called ujamaa villages. The goal of the project was to increase the participation of pastoralists in the market economy. Reining was asked to make judgements about a number of different areas including the social suitability of the ujamaa approach and program participation recruitment criteria.

268-270 ANTHROPOLOGY IN USE

Husain, Tariq
1976   Use of Anthropologists in Project Appraisal by the World
        Bank. In Development from Below Anthropologists and
        Development Situations. David C. Pitt (ed.), the Hague:
        Mouton Publishers.

268   JAMAICA   1972

Adam Kuper was employed as a planner by the National Planning
Agency in the Office of the Prime Minister, Jamaica. His main
concern was to combat urban unemployment as well as to raise rural
productivity.

Kuper, Adam
1974   Critical applied anthropology: Urban unemployment and
        rural productivity in Jamaica. Ethnos. 39:7-26.

269   UNITED STATES   1972

The Tucson Garbage Research Project was begun. This project developed
out of a graduate student seminar in archeology at the University
of Arizona. Its initial concern was the contrast between stereo-
types held concerning various community group, e.g. low-income
families and their real behavior. The methodology used included
the descriptive analysis of random samples of household waste drawn
from Tucson, Arizona.

The project has provided data to various "policy-relevant"
organizations like the General Accounting Office and the U. S.
Senate's Select Committee on Nutrition and Human Needs. The primary
focus of the project's policy relevant aspects is the nature of
food waste and the behavior patterns associated with it. The project
is being replicated in Milwaukee.

National Science Foundation
1979   Archaeology Reconstructs the Present. Mosaic.
        10(1):30-37.

270   UNITED STATES   1972

Physical anthropologist Christine Cronk was employed by the Developmental Evaluation Clinic, Children's Hospital, Medical Center in
Boston, Massachusetts as a member of an interdisciplinary team
diagnosing and recommending treatment for mentally retarded children.
Using anthroposcopy and anthropometry, she carried out phenotypic
and growth assessment of children suspected of mental retardation
to determine if they have abnormal phenotypes. In addition, she conducted a longitudinal study of Down's syndrome children, collaborating
with a nutritionist in order to monitor their well being and regulate
their diet.

Cronk, Christine E.
1976   Statural growth in Down's Syndrome children, birth
        to three years. American Journal of Physical
        Anthropology. 44:173.

1976   Physical growth. In A Manual for Home Training Special-
        ists of the Multihandicapped Child, Massachusetts
        Department of Mental Health.

271 SWITZERLAND   1972

The World Health Organization Task Force Planning Meeting on
the Acceptability of Fertility Regulating Methods was organized
with the backing of medical researchers as well as demographer
J. C. Caldwell. Among the participants were three anthropologists,
Haydee Seijas, Masri Singaribun and Steven Polgar.

Polgar, Steven and J. F. Marshall
1976   The Search for Culturally Acceptable Fertility
        Regulating Methods. In Culture, Natality and Family
        Planning. Steven Polgar and J. F. Marshall (eds.),
        Carolina Population Center Monograph 21, Chapel Hill,
        N. C.

272 UNITED STATES   1973

The concept of social network seems to have developed primarily
within anthropology. Unfortunately its use in applied situations
is infrequently documented. One example of its use was a study
done by Alvin W. Wolfe on the effects of social network on employment. The study compared social networks of those successfully employed and those who weren't. The study did not find
significant differences between the two groups.

Wolfe, Alvin W. with Linda Whileford Dean
1974   Social Network Effects on Employment. Report submitted
        to the Manpower Administration, U. S. Department of
        Labor.

273 UNITED STATES   1972

In the aftermath of the Attica prison riots anthropologist Frank
J. Salamone was hired to develop a course for Attica prison
guards in "Conflict Resolution." Under substantial administrative
controls the course of study had limited success.

Salamone, Frank J.
1977   The Attica Human Relations Course: An Example of
        Leaping before Looking. Anthropology and Education
        Quarterly. 8(4):227-229.

274   UNITED STATES   1972

   Three anthropologists enter the field of "Social Impact
   Assessment" required of all federal agencies under the National
   Environmental Policy Act of 1969. Magoroh Maruyama became
   Resident Social Scientist with the U. S. Corps of Engineers
   in Washington, D. C., and began participating in the Corps'
   formulation of its social impact assessment guidelines and
   instructions. Maruyama also invited Sue-Ellen Jacobs and
   Anthony Wilden as consultants to a series of meetings. In
   1973 Maruyama formed a social science consultant team which
   included anthropologists Sue-Ellen Jacobs and John H. Peterson.

   Maruyama, Magorah
   1973   Cultural, Social and Psychological Considerations
             in the Planning of Public Works. Technological
             Forecasting and Social Change, 5:135-143.

   Vlachos, Evan (ed.)
   1975   Social Impact Assessment: An Overview. Corps of
             Engineers, 1WR Paper 75-P7.

275   UNITED STATES   1972

   The High School Social Organization study program was initiated
   by Francis A. J. Ianni. The project had both theoretical and
   applied orientations and used a variety of data gathering
   techniques. Out of these research efforts come information useful for school programs. The project dealt with various types
   of schools in the New York metropolitan area.

   Calhoun, Craig Jackson
   1974   General Status: Specific Role. Council on Anthro-
             pology and Education Quarterly, 5(2):16-20.

   Iaani, Francis A. J.
   1974   Social Organization Study Program: An Interim Report.
             5(2):1-8.

   Varenne, Herve
   1974   From Grading and Freedom of Choice to Ranking and
             Segregation in an American High School. Council
             on Anthropology and Education Quarterly, 5(2):9-15.

276   UNITED STATES   1972

   Anthropologists were evaluation researchers for United States
   Office of Education rural school development projects. Much
   of this work was carried out through the Cambridge, Massachusetts,
   consulting firm, Abt Associates, Inc.

Burns, Allan
1975   An Anthropologist at Work: Field Perspectives on Applied Ethnography. Council on Anthropology and Education Quarterly. 6(4):28-33.

Clinton, Charles A.
1975   The Anthropologist as Hired Hand, Human Organization, 34(2):197-204.

1975   A Social and Educational History of Hancock County, Kentucky, Hawesville, Kentucky: Bruner Printing Company.

1976   On Bargaining with the Devil: Contract Ethnography and Accountability in Fieldwork. Council on Anthropology and Education Quarterly. 8(2):25-28.

1977   A Social and Education History of Hancock County Kentucky. In Rural America: A Social and Educational History of Ten Communities. Stephen J. Fitzsimmons, Peter C. Folff, and Abby J. Freeman (eds.), New York: Basic Books.

Everhart, Robert B.
1975   Problems of Doing Fieldwork in Educational Evaluation. Human Organization. 34(2):205-215.

Fitzsimmons, Stephen J.
1975   The Anthropologist in a Strange Land. Human Organization, 34(2):183-196.

277 MICRONESIA   1972

The United States Department of Defense planned to carry out seismic testing on the island of Enewetak. This island had been the home of a native population prior to Atomic Weapons testing carried out in 1947. The seismic testing was to further disturb the natural environment. The seismic testing program referred to as PACE (Pacific Cratering Experiments) was actively resisted through the legal use of provisions of the National Environmental Policy Act (NEPA). Anthropologist Robert C. Kiste, who had had considerable experience in Micronesian ethnography was requested by the Micronesian Legal Services Corporation to serve as a witness in the hearings. Kiste's activities very clearly advocated the interests of the Enewetak people and contributed to their successful resistance.

Hines, Neal O.
1962   Proving Ground: An Account of the Radiobiological Studies in the Pacific, 1946-1961. Seattle: University of Washington Press.

Kiste, Robert C.
1976   The People of Enewetak atoll vs. The U. S. Department
        of Defense. In Dilemmas in Fieldwork, Ethics and
        Anthropology. Michael A. Rynkiewich and James P.
        Spradley, (eds.) New York: Wiley.

Tobin, Jack A.
1967   The Resettlement of the Enewetak People: A Study of
        a Dispaced Community in the Marshall Islands. Unpub-
        lished Ph.D. dissertation, University of California.

278   UNITED STATES   1973

Anthropologists come to be involved in the analysis of the
impact of power production on the Navajo Reservation population.
Referred to as the Lake Powell Project this effort involved
anthropologists, Jerrold E. Levy and Donald G. Callaway.

Callaway, Donald G., Jerrold E. Levy and Eric Henderson
1976   The effects of Power Production and Strip Mining
        on Local Navajo Populations. Lake Powell Research
        Bulletin No. 22, Los Angeles: Institute of Geophysics
        and Planetary Physics. University of California,
        Los Angeles.

279   UNITED STATES   1973

Acquinas College a small Catholic School in a deteriorating
neighborhood of Grand Rapids, Michigan attempted to stimulate
various kinds of development in the surrounding neighborhood.
Eastown, as the area was called, was undergoing rapid decay in
the quality of community life and facilities. The Eastown project
involved persons of various disciplinary backgrounds including
anthropology. The techniques used in the project were diverse,
but did not involve both research and action. Linda Elaine
Easley was the anthropologist involved.

Easley, Linda Elaine, Thomas Whitfield Edison and Michael Ronan
Williams
1978   Eastown! A Report on How Aquinas College Helped its
        Local Community Reverse Neighborhood Transition and
        Deterioration. Battlecreek, MI: W. K. Kellogg Foundation.

280   UNITED STATES   1973

Under contract to the Department of Housing and Urban Development,
anthropologists Theodore Downing and Thomas Weaver served as
researchers in a project to assess the business management
practices and political organization of seven Arizona Indian
reservations. The groups were Cocopah, Ak Chin, Fort McDowell,
Camp Verde, Hualapai, Payson-Apache and Havasupai.

Weaver, Thomas and Theodore Downing
1974   Office Procedures Manual for Seven Arizona Indian
        Reservations, Report of the Seven Reservations
        Project. Tucson: Bureau of Ethnic Research,
        University of Arizona.

1974   The Tribal Management Procedures Study Report of
        the Seven Reservations Project. Tucson: Bureau of
        Ethnic Research, University of Arizona

281 ECUADOR   1973

The U. S. Agency for International Development sponsored
assistance for the planning of metropolitan Quito. Lisa R.
Peattie was an anthropological consultant in this case.

Peattie, Lisa R.
1973   Social Aspects of Planning for the Metropolitan
        Area of Quito. Washington, D. C.: U. S. Agency
        for International Development.

282 UNITED STATES   1973

Using the rehabilitation of a community center and the creation
of a new park/playground as a catalyst for group organization,
the transferability of the Vicos Community development strategy
was tested in the Watts section of Los Angeles. Anthropologist
Robert M. Wulff was a member of the U. S. Army Reserve which
carried out the project as a Domestic Action Program. Wulff
served as a community development specialist supervising a team
of reservists. He also acted as a community liason with the
Army. The strategy of slowly sharing power and expertise was
evaluated as successful.

Wulff, Robert M.
1977   Vicos in Watts: Testing Anthropological Change
        Strategies in Urban America. ERIC Microfiche
        (Abstracted in Resources in Education) Princeton, NJ:
        Educational Testing Service.

283 UNITED STATES   1973

The Foreign Assistance Act of 1973 provided for "social soundness
analysis" of overseas development projects. This dramatically
increased the number of "contract" and "direct hire" opportunities
for anthropologists in the Agency for International Development.
Social Soundness Analysis focuses on cultural compatibility,
diffusion of benefits and extensiveness of impacts.

U. S. Agency for International Development
1975   Handbook 3, Project Assistance. Washington, D. C.:
        U. S. A.I.D.

284-286 ANTHROPOLOGY IN USE

284   UNITED STATES   1973

In 1973 the Institute for Social Science Research at the
University of Montana began a research project to determine
the social impact of the extraction of coal resources in the
Northern Great Plains. The research made use of anthropological
techniques. Data was gathered in and around Colstrip, Montana;
Gillette, Wyoming and Stanton, North Dakota. Impact was
assessed as it occurred.

Institute for Social Science Research
1974   A Comparative Case Study of the Impact of Coal
          Development on the Way of Life of People in the Coal
          Areas of Eastern Montana and Northeastern Wyoming,
          Final Report. Missoula, Montana: Institute for
          Social Science Research, University of Montana.

285   CANADA   1973

An oil company consortium called Panarctic Oils, LTD. began
seismic surveying in an area of Bathurst Island used by an
Eskimo community for caribou hunting. The search for oil had
a significant negative impact on wildlife resources. This
caused representatives of the community to petition the
Ministry of Indian and Northern Affairs to reexamine their
policies concerning oil exploration. Anthropologist Milton
M. R. Freeman worked as an advisor to the Eskimo community.
Freeman provided information and evaluation which was useful
to the community's position.

Freeman, Milton M. R.
1977   Anthropologists and Policy-Relevant Research the
          Case for Accountability. In Applied Anthropology
          in Canada, Proceedings No. 4, of the Canadian
          Ethnology Society, Hamilton, Ontario: Canadian
          Ethnology Society.

286   UNITED STATES   1973

The Bureau of Ethnic Research, Department of Anthropology,
University of Arizona initiated a comprehensive survey of
housing conditions of Douglas, Arizona under a Bureau of Community
and Environmental Management, United States Public Health Service
contract. The project was directed by Thomas Weaver. Data analysis
was under the supervision of Theodore Downing.

Weaver, Thomas and Theodore Downing (eds.)
1975   The Douglas Report: The Community Context of Housing
          and Social Problems. Tucson: Bureau of Ethnic Research,
          University of Arizona.

287 UNITED STATES   1973

   Anthropologists working in conjunction with Abt Associates,
   Inc., a Cambridge, Massachusetts consulting firm were part of
   a team which carried out an evaluation of components of a so-called
   housing allowance program instigated by the Department of Housing
   and Urban Development. The component focused upon was the
   administrative agency experiment which evaluated a model administrative structure.

   Chambers, Erve J.
       Working for the Man: The Anthropologist in Policy-
       Relevant Research. Human Organization. 36(3):258-267.

288 CANADA   1973

   The Hobbema Curriculum project was designed to bring about
   locally controlled change among four native Canadian groups
   in Alberta. The project was calculated to produce new and
   appropriate curriculum materials. The project made use of
   the concepts of devolution and deconcentration.

   Aoki, T.
   1973   Toward Devolution in the Control of Education on a
           Native Reserve in Alberta. The Hobbema Curriculum
           Story. Council on Anthropology and Education News-
           letter, 4(2):1-6.

289 UNITED STATES   1973

   Anthropological research techniques are used to provide data
   concerning Navajo desires in public school architecture and
   design. Working with the sanction of the local Navajo school
   board and through a California architectural firm, the research
   helped achieve a school design which was enthusiastically accepted
   by community members.

   Clement, Dorothy C.
   1976   Cognitive Anthropology and Applied Problems in Education.
           Do Applied Anthropologists Apply Anthropology?, M.
           Angrosino, (ed.) Proceedings of the Southern Anthropological
           Society, No. 10. Athens: University of Georgia Press.

   Harding, Joe R.
   1973   An Architectural Planning Study: Prospective User
           Perceptions (Form and Functions) of the Proposed Ramah
           Navajo Learning Center. Berkeley: Policy Research
           and Planning Group.

290 UNITED STATES   1974

   Allen C. Turner developed a program based upon principles derived
   from the Research and Development approach, which was to lead
   to development among the Southern Paiute at near Kaibab, Utah.
   Turner worked with Band leadership on various policy research
   activities.

   Turner, Allen C.
   1974   Southern Paiute Research and Development Program, A
             Pre-Proposal. Cedar City, Utah: Southern Utah
             State College.

291 UNITED STATES   1974

   The Society of Professional Anthropologists was formed in
   Tucson, Arizona. SOPA's primary goals are to provide service
   and support to non-academically employed anthropologists in
   southern Arizona. SOPA officials have organized workshops at
   both the 1975 and 1976 meetings of the American Anthropological
   Association. Services provided include information on job
   seeking strategies, theoretical up-date sessions for nonacademic anthropologists, and information on national political
   developments. Following SOPA's lead similar organizations
   developed in Washington and Chicago.

   Bainton, R. Barry
   1975   Society of Professional Anthropologists formed in
             Tucson. Anthropology Newsletter. 16(8):4-6.

292 UNITED STATES   1974

   The passage of the National Environmental Policy Act of 1969
   stimulated a substantial amount of related legislation requiring
   social impact assessment. One of the NEPA progency having this
   effect was the Community Development Act of 1974 (PL 93-383).
   The Community Development Act requires that there be an assessment
   of the social impact of expenditures under the act. William
   Millsap carried out such an assessment in a small Texas
   community.

   Millsap, William
   1978   New Tools for an Old Trade: Social Impact Assessment in
             Community and Regional Development. In Social Science
             Education for Development. William T. Vickers and
             Glenn R. Howze (eds.) Tuskegee Institute, Center for
             Rural Development. Tuskegee Institute, Alabama.

293 GREAT BRITAIN   1974

   Although the legislative mandate is not as clear as in the
   United States environmental impact assessment is also practiced
   in Great Britain. Anthropologists are staff members of the Project
   Appraisal for Development Control group at the University of

Aberdeen. This group has been working in environmental impact
assessment since 1974.

Bisset, Ronald
1978   Environmental Impact Analysis: A Review Article.
          Royal Anthropological Institute News. (26):1-4.

Clark, B. D., K. Chapman, Ronald Bisset, and P. Wathern
1978   Methods of Environmental Impact Analysis, Built
          Environment. 4(1):111-121.

UNITED STATES   1974

Anthropologists as well as other behavioral scientists come to be
involved in various evaluation projects as associates of the Center
for New Schools in Chicago. The primary effort was the Documentation
and Technical Assistance in Urban Schools Project. This was based
on a $4.5 million dollar contract with the National Institute of
Education. The project is exploratory and is based on the "observed
day-to-day realities of urban public school life." Research is being
carried out in a number of sites in New York City, Los Angeles,
CA., Louisville, Ky., San Jose, CA., Washington, D.C. and
Minneapolis. MN. Anthropologists participating in project operations
include Norris Brock Johnson, Woodrow W. Clark, Steven Sherlock,
and Lillian B. Paoli.

Center for New Schools
1977   DTA Project, Overview 1977. Chicago: Center for New
          Schools.

UNITED STATES   1974

Sue-Ellen Jacobs was retained as part of a team which engaged in
social impact assessment for the Springer-Sangamon Environmental
Research Program of an Army Corps of Engineers reservoir project
on the Sangamon River in central Illinois. Jacobs later participated
in the development of guidelines for evaluating other Army Corps of
Engineer projects.

Jacobs, Sue-Ellen, Barbara A. Schleicher and Raymond A. Ontiveros
1974   Preliminary Social and Cultural Profiles of the Human
          Communities in the Springer-Sangamon Impact Zones,
          Social Impact Assessment and Identification of Resource-
          Oriented Attributes of the Human Environment in the
          Springer-Sangamon Impact Zones - Phase 1. In Bell, D.T.
          and F. L. Johnson (eds.) Annual Report FY74 for the
          Springer-Sangamon Environmental Research Program,
          Department of Forestry and Illinois Agricultural Experiment
          Station University of Illinois, Urbana - Champaign, Ill.

296   UNITED STATES   1975

Anthropologist Magoroh Maruyama was engaged by the National Aeronautics and Space Administration to initiate research leading to optimum extraterrestrial community design. Much of this was carried out at the NASA/Stanford Summer Study of Space Colonization. Maruyama also has written on urban planning.

Maruyama, Magoroh
1976   Extraterrestrial Community Design. Psychological and Cultural Consideration. Cybernetica. 19:45-62.

297   UNITED STATES   1975

The Wyoming Human Services Project was created to deal with the human problems which have developed in Wyoming communities as a result of the rapid development of energy resources in the state. The project, which is multidisciplinary, attempted to provide "human service teams" in the coal communities of Gillette and Wheatland. These teams have worked in public administration, legal services, public health nursing, recreation services, community mental health, youth services, gerontology services and community education.

Uhlman, Julie M.
1977a   Anthropologists in a Multidisciplinary Training Program. Presented at the Houston, TX meetings of the American Anthropological Association.

1977b   The Delivery of Human Services in Wyoming Boomtowns. In Socio-Economic Impact of Western Energy Development. Berry Crawford and Edward H. Allen (eds.) Ann Arbor: Science Publishers

Uhlman, Julie M., Robert Kimble and David Throgmorton
1976   A Study of Two Wyoming Communities Undergoing the Initial Effects of Energy Resource Development. In The Powder River Basin: Buffalo and Douglas, Wyoming - 1975. Report prepared for the Wyoming Department of Economic Planning and Development. (Mimeo)

298   UNITED STATES   1975

The Anthropology Resource Center was established as one of the first public-interest anthropology organizations in the United States. This type of anthropology, "differs from traditional applied anthropology in what is considered the object of study, whose interests the researcher represents, and what the researcher does with the results of his or her work. Public-interest anthropology grows out of the democratic traditions of citizen activism rather than the bureaucratic needs of management and control. It is based on the premise that social problems-war, poverty, racism, sexism, environmental degradation misuse of technology-are deeply rooted in social structure, and the role of the intellectual is to work with citizens in promoting fundamental social change (1979:5)".

Davis, Shelton H. and Robert O. Mathews
1979   Anthropological Resource Center: Public Interest
        Anthropology - Beyond the Bureaucratic Ethos. Practicing
        Anthropology. 1(3):5,25-26.

Nader, Ralph
1975   Anthropology in Law and Civic Action. In Anthropology
        and Society. Bela C. Maday (ed.) Washington, D. C.:
        Anthropological Society of Washington.

299   UNITED STATES   1975

In the 1970's there emerged a general downturn in the amount of
academic opportunity for anthropologists. This fact was most
clearly demonstrated by research published by R. G. D'Andrade, E. A.
Hammel, D. L. Adkins and C.K. McDaniel on the demographics of
Ph.D.'s supplied and teaching services demanded. They state, "our
most optimistic assessment of the future of academic employment in
anthropology indicates that after 1982 over two-thirds of all
anthropology Ph.D.'s will have to find employment outside academia"
(1975:772).

Balderston, F. E. and Roy Radner
1971   Academic Demand for New Ph.D.'s 1970-90: Its Sensitivity
        to Alternate Policies. Paper P-26. Ford Foundation
        Program in University Administration. University of
        California, Berkeley.

Cartter, Alan M.
1974   The Academic Labor Market. In Higher Education and the
        Labor Market. M. S. Gordon (ed.) New York: McGraw-Hill.

D'Andrade, R. G., E. A. Hammel, D. L. Adkins, and C. K. McDaniel
1975   Academic Opportunity in Anthropology 1974-90. American
        Anthropologist. 77(4):753-773.

300   UNITED STATES   1975

Larry Naylor contracted with the Bureau of Indian Affairs to research
Alaska Native employment on the Trans-Alaska Oil Pipeline. The
support of this project was later expanded to include other government
agencies and private sector groups such as Alyeska (Trans-Alaska Oil
Pipeline Service Company).

Naylor, Larry L.
1976   Native Hire on Trans-Alaska Pipeline. Report prepared
        for Arctic Gas Pipeline Company, Department of Anthropology,
        University of Alaska.

301-304 ANTHROPOLOGY IN USE

301 UNITED STATES 1975

Development in Alaska stimulated various types of policy studies. These include Nancy Yaw Davis's work with land use. Her efforts were intended to increase understanding of rural Alaskan culture change as this related to policy issues identified by the Federal-State Land Use Planning Commission. These issues included change and stability in subsistence activities, effects of cash-jobs, intra village and village government communication and social change. The research methodology employed a survey designed in consultation with community members.

David, Nancy Yaw
1976 Steps Toward Understanding Rapid Culture Change in Native Rural Alaska. Federal-State Land Use Planning Commission for Alaska Study Number 16.

302 UNITED STATES 1975

According to one of its most vocal proponents, Ailon Shiloh, the first reference to therapeutic anthropology in print was in a discussion of the question, "what is applied anthropology?" developed by Alvin W. Wolfe published in Human Organization. Shiloh suggests that therapeutic anthropologists receive special training and become a kind of health professional which actually treats patients.

Anonymous
1975 What is Applied Anthropology? Human Organization. 34:370.

Shiloh, Ailon
1977 Therapeutic Anthropology: The Anthropologist as Private Practitioner. American Anthropologist. 79(2):443-445.

303 UNITED STATES 1975

The United States Public Health Service contracted Joe R. Harding to assist in developing methodologies for determining the acceptability of hearing aid use at Zuni Pueblo, New Mexico.

Harding, Joe R. and Jefferson Boyer
1976 Determination of Zuni Perceptions of Otitis Media Treatments and Attributes: A Methodology and Some Pilot Results. Chapel Hill, N. C.: Policy Research and Planning Group.

304 MOROCCO 1975

The Food and Agriculture Organization (FAO) organized a seminar in Tangiers focused upon agricultural planning and population in developing Francophone Africa and the role of anthropology in development.

de Garine, I.
1978   Population, Production, and Culture in the Plains
        Societies of Northern Cameroon and Chad: The
        Anthropologist in Development Projects. Current
        Anthropology19(1):42-65.

305   UNITED STATES   1975

      Sue-Ellen Jacobs carried out a Social Impact Assessment for the
      Bureau of Reclamation. The zone of impact was to include
      portions of the Rio Grande-Española Valley in New Mexico. Impact
      zone inhabitants included both Spanish Americans and American
      Indians.

      Jacobs, Sue-Ellen
      1977   Social Impact Assessment: Experiences in Evaluation
              Research, Applied Anthropology and Human Ethics.
              Mississippi State University Occasional Papers
              in Anthropology. John H. Peterson (ed.) Department of
              Anthropology, Mississippi State University.

306   UNITED STATES   1975

      Under the auspices of the Tampa Metropolitan Development Agency
      and Department of Recreation, Robert M. Wulff evaluated two
      recreation facilities: a new playground and the city's system of
      18 community recreation centers. Both studies took a user-oriented
      approach to recreation service delivery identifying user/emic view
      contrasted to planner/etic view of the services. Inconsistencies in
      the two views were discovered.

      Wulff, Robert M.
      1976   Tampa's Community Centers: An Analysis of Recreation
              Programming and Policy. Tampa, Florida: Human Resources
              Institute and Center of Applied Anthropology, University
              of South Florida.

307   PERU   1976

      The International Potato Center, using direct hire social scientists
      including anthropologists began research on farming practices in
      the Mantaro Valley. The valley is the largest agricultural area
      of Central Andes region of Peru. According to Werge, "the primary
      purpose was to provide baseline data on technical and socio-economic
      constraints to potato production which might help to orient the
      agricultural investigation at [the center] toward appropriate
      technologies." Research projects on indigenous storage and processing
      technology have been carried out.

      Werge, Robert W.
      1977   Potato Storage Systems in the Mantaro Valley of Peru.
              Lima: Centro Internacional de la Papa.

Werge, Robert W. and Marisela Benavides
1979   Investigation of Farming in Peru by Means of a Multi-Visit Survey. Paper presented at the Society for Applied Anthropology at Philadelphia.

Werge, Robert W. and G. Frerks
1978   Evaluation of Solar Dehydration Techniques. Lima: Centro International de la Papa.

Werge, Robert W. and G. Frerks
1977   Potato Processing in the Central Highlands of Peru, CIP Social Science Unit, Thrust VIII, Lima: Centro Internacional de la Papa.

308   UNITED STATES   1976

The United States Agency for International Development organized a conference focused on rural life in Afghanistan to be held at the University of Nebraska-Omaha. The conferees were concerned with potentials for development. This effort was somewhat related to the new directions for development brought about by the Foreign Assistance Act of 1973. Anthropologists involved included Jon Anderson, Asen Balikci, Robert Canfield, Louis Dupree, Nancy Dupree, Lincoln Keiser, and Nazif Shahrani.

Dupree, Louis
1977   'USAID' and Social Scientists Discuss Afghanistan's Development Prospects. American Universities Field Staff Reports, South Asia Series. 21(2).

309   UNITED STATES   1976

As part of an attempt to develop a strategy for dealing with the development problems of the Sahel, the Agency for International Development contracted with David W. Brokensha, Michael M. Horowitz and Thayer Scudder to develop a research prospectus for the region. They proposed a long-term, multicomponent study lasting over 15 to 25 years. Some of the areas of research stressed were farming systems, social soundness analysis of dams, marketing systems, and various topics relating to health.

Brokensha, David W., Michael M. Horowitz and Thayer Scudder
1977   The Anthropology of Rural Development in the Sahel. Binghamton, NY: Institute for Development Anthropology.

310   UNITED STATES   1976

A group of young anthropologists led by Karen L. Michaelson assessed the impact of the planned construction of Interstate 88 in up-state New York. The assessment was supported as a student-originated-study project of the National Science Foundation.

Van Tassell, Jon and Karen L. Michaelson
1977   Social Impact Assessment: Methods and Practice, (Interstate 88 in New York). (Final Report: National Science Foundation, Student-Originated-Study Grant, Summer, 1976), Binghamton: NY: Department of Anthropology, SUNY, Binghamton.

311 UNITED STATES   1976

The Minnesota Work Equity Program was funded by the United States Department of Labor to demonstrate an approach to Welfare reform involving required participation in work or work training programs. The evaluation of this social experiment has been carried out by Abt Associates, Inc. with the participation of three anthropologists as field workers. Trend notes, "We tried to steer a middle course between having the field-workers do free-form, "lone wolf" ethnography and making them into mere data gatherers, the go-fers of the economists and survey analysts   (1978:399)."

Trend, M. G.
1978   Research in Progress: The Minnesota Work Equity Project Evaluation. Human Organization. 37(4):398-399.

312 UNITED STATES   1976

The Center for New Schools organized a project to evaluate an innovative education project in Cleveland Heights, Ohio. The approach was consistent with traditional ethnography in that it relied heavily on participant observation.

Wilson, Stephen
1977   The Use of Ethnographic Methods in Educational Evaluation. Human Organization. 36(2):200-203.

313 UNITED STATES   1977

The World Bank sponsored a research project entitled, "Appropriate Technology for Water Supply and Waste Disposal in Developing Countries." within the Energy, Water and Telecommunications Department. Directed by Mary Elmendorf and Patricia K. Buckles, the project used the case study method to analyze, "the choice, adoption, and diffusion of technological innovations for water supply and excreta disposal." The project collected case materials in Guatemala, Mexico, El Salvador, Colombia, Nicaragua, and Haiti. The project made use of both structured and unstructured research techniques.

Elmendorf, Mary and Patricia K. Buckles
1978   Socio-cultural Aspects of Water Supply and Excreta Disposal. The World Bank, Energy, Water and Telecommunications Department, Public Utilities Notes (P.U. Report No. RES 15) Washington, D. C.: The World Bank.

UNITED STATES 1977

The Cross-Cultural Resource Center of California State University, Sacramento was proposed for federal funding submitted to the Office of Bilingual Education under the Bilingual Education Act (PL 93-380). This project proposal was developed by Steven F. Arvizu and others and was funded. Its major goal was to, "support training to improve the likelihood of success in programs of bilingual education" in a region which included Arizona, California and Nevada as well as some Pacific Territories.

Arvizu, Steven F.
1978   Home-School Linkages: A Cross Cultural Approach to Parent Participation. In A Cultural Approach to Parent Participation. (Bilingual Education Training Series) Sacramento: Cross Cultural Resource Center.

Arvizu, Steven F. and Warren A. Snyder with Paul T. Espinosa
1978   Demystifying the Concept of Culture: Theoretical and Conceptual Tools Monograph I. (Bilingual Education Training Series). Sacramento: Cross Cultural Resource Center.

Gibson, Margaret A. and Steven F. Arvizu
1978   Demystifying the Concept of Culture: Theoretical and Conceptual Tools Monograph II. (Bilingual Education Training Series). Sacramento: Cross Cultural Resource Center.

Gil, Abjandra
1978   The Changing Role Definition among Chicanas Revealed Through Life History Technique. In A Cultural Approach to Parent Participation. (Bilingual Education Training Series). Sacramento: Cross Cultural Resource Center.

Guzmán de Velasco, Isabel
1978   A Guide for Effective Parent and Community Participation in Bilingual Bicultural Education. In A Cultural Approach to Parent Participation. (Bilingual Education Training Series). Sacramento, CA: Cross Cultural Resource Center.

Isáis, Raoul
1978   A Minority Perspective on a Cultural Approach to Parent Participation in Bilingual Cross Cultural Education. In A Cultural Approach to Parent Participation. (Bilingual Education Training Series). Sacramento: Cross Cultural Resource Center.

Ogbu, John U.
1978   Cross Cultural Resource Center Institute on Parent Participation. An Evaluation Report. (Bilingual Education Training Series). Sacramento: Cross Cultural Resource Center.

Rich, George W. and Margaret A. Gibson
1978   Demystifying the Concept of Culture: A Teacher's Guide
        to the Cross- cultural Study of Games and Play, Monograph
        IV. (Bilingual Education Training Series). Sacramento:
        Cross Cultural Resource Center.

315 UNITED STATES   1977

As part of a multi-disciplinary team anthropologists Erve Chambers,
Charles A. Clinton and John H. Peterson, Jr. field tested the WRAM
(Water Resources Assessment Methodology) Procedure which had
been developed at the U. S. Army Engineer Waterways Experiment
Station, Vicksburg, Mississippi. The field test was carried out in
the Tensas River Valley in Louisiana.

Clinton, Charles A. (ed.)
1978   Social Impact Assessment in Context: The Tensas Documents.
        Occasional Papers in Anthropology, Mississippi State
        University, Mississippi State, Mississippi.

Solomon, R. Charles, Billy K. Colfert, William J. Hansen,
Sue E. Richardson, Larry W. Canter and Evan G. Vlachos
1977   Water Resources Assessment Methodology (WRAM - Impact
        Assessment and Alternative Evaluation, Report Y-77-1),
        Vicksburg, Mississippi: Environmental Effects Laboratory,
        U. S. Army Engineer Waterways Experiment.

316 UNITED STATES   1977

The Agency for International Development convened a workshop which
focused primarily upon the development of recommendations concerning
the use of "Social Soundness Analysis" in the international development
arena.

McPherson, Laura (ed.)
1978   The Role of Anthropology in the Agency for International
        Development. Binghamton, NY: Institute for Development
        Anthropology, Inc.

317 TANZANIA   1977

Alan H. Jacobs had done ethnographic field work in Maasai country
in Tanzania in the period 1956-58. He was contracted by U. S.
Agency for International Development to do a 26 day field study
in 1977. The report was to address three issues. These are,
"what major changes have occurred in Maasailand and in Maasai lifeways
over the past 20 years?, What does the future hold for their culture and
economic base? and what development inputs can best be made to assist

the Maasai in entering into the mainstream of modern Tanzanian life? (Jacobs, 1978:2)." Jacobs report summarized his perceptions of 20 years of change, his projections about the future and his specific recommendations

Jacobs, Alan H.
1978   Development in Tanzania Maasailand: The Perspective over 20 years, 1957-1977, (Contr. No. Afr-C-1279). U.S. A.I.D. Mission in Tanzania.

318   UNITED STATES   1977

Pan American Health Organization (PAHO) sponsored a workshop entitled, "Modern Medicine and Medical Anthropology in the Border Population," in El Paso, Texas. The workshop produced a series of recommendations concerning PAHOS policy primarily as it deals with the relationship between modern and traditional medical systems.

Pan American Health Organization
1978   Selected Bibliography in Medical Anthropology for Health Professionals in the Americas. El Paso, TX: Field Office, Pan American Health Organization.

Velimirovic, Boris (ed.)
1978   Modern Medicine and Medical Anthropology in the United States Mexico Border Population. Proceedings of a Workshop held in El Paso, TX. (January 20-21, 1977). Scientific Publication No. 359, Pan American Health Organization, Pan American Sanitary Bureau Regional Office of the World Health Organization 525 Twenty-third Street, N. W. Washington, D. C. 20037.

319   UNITED STATES   1978

The Committee on International Relations' Subcommittee on International Development of the U. S. House of Representatives held a briefing on the impact of rapid economic development on native peoples of the Amazon. Included in the record of the briefing were comments by Shelton Davis who is director of the Anthropology Resource Center. His testimony made reference to devastating effect that highway, agricultural and industrial development will have on native Amazonian peoples. Davis also spoke to the fact that the massive social and ecological destruction was the responsibility of an alliance between Brazil's military government and a number of large multinational corporations.

Davis, Shelton H.
1977   Victims of the Miracle: Development and the Indians of Brazil. London: Cambridge University Press.

Davis, Shelton H.
1978   Briefing on Impact of Brazil's 'Economic Miracle' on the
        Amazonian Indians. Hearing before the Subcommittee on
        International Development of the Committee on International
        Relations. (House of Representatives, Ninety-Fifth Congress)

Davis, Shelton H. and Robert O. Mathews
1976   The Geological Imperative: Anthropology and Development
        in the Amazon Basin of South America. Anthropology
        Resource Center: Cambridge, MA.

320   UNITED STATES   1978

Fairbanks, Alaska was subject to certain impact due to the construction of the Trans-Alaska Pipeline. In response to impact problems the Impact Information Center was established. The staff included anthropologist Mim Dixon.

Dixon, Mim
1978   What Happened to Fairbanks? The Effects of the Trans-
        Alaska Oil Pipeline on the Community of Fairbanks, Alaska.
        The Social Impact Assessment Series, No. 1. Boulder, CO:
        Westview Press.

321   UNITED STATES   1978

Using what he refers to as an Action Anthropology approach Donald D. Stull started a project with the Kansas Kickapoo. The project produced linguistic research data which may be used in bilingual/bicultural programs in the future. This is to be supplemented by general research on Kickapoo ethnography. These activities are supported by the Tribal Council and has resulted in tangible benefits for the tribe. The ethnographic component of the research has resulted in a multimedia exhibit on traditions and change; improved historical documentation for the tribe and various planned publications. Stull notes some of the same problems the Schlesier had with his Southern Cheyenne work, that is difficulty in attracting foundation funding.

Stull, Donald D.
1979   Action Anthropology among the Kansas Kickapoo, Paper
        presented at the Society for Applied Anthropology meetings
        at Philadelphia.

322   PARAGUAY   1978

David Maybury-Lewis was requested by U. S. Agency for International Development to investigate the conditions of Indians there and to determine if development funds could assist them. He visited various Indian sites and submitted a report to A.I.D. This survey dealt with a number of issues including accusations of Paraguayan government complicity in the raiding and murder of Indians there.

Cultural Survival, inc.
1979   Paraguayan Update. Cultural Survival Newsletter
        3(2):1-2.

GENERAL INDEX

Aba Riots 58.
Aberle, David F. 106, 134.
Aborigines Protection Society 5.
Abt Associates, Inc. 276, 287, 311.
Acculturation 11.
Acquinas College 279.
Action Anthropology 133, 170, 204, 240, 261.
Action Research 94, 219, 244.
Adair, John 139, 184.
Adams, Harold S. 187.
Adams, Richard N. 159, 201.
Adat Law 40, 64.
Adelman, Irma 206.
Adkins, D. L. 299.
Advocacy Planning 230, 236.
Agency for Internation Development 164, 209, 217, 249, 281, 283, 308, 309, 316, 317, 322.
Agricultural Development 167, 195, 229, 234, 256, 304, 307, 317.
Aiyappan, A. 135.
Alcoholism 241.
Alers, Oscar J. 168.
Allen, W. 114.
Amazon 319.
American Anthropological Association 90, 154, 232, 249, 291.
American Blacks 259, 262.
American Civil Liberties Union 118.
American Ethnological Society 6.
American Friends Service Committee 74.
American Indian Chicago Conference 204.
American Indian Movement 247.
American Indians 6, 7, 11, 14, 16, 19, 68, 70, 79, 88, 104, 133, 202, 204, 205, 207, 212, 223, 224, 231, 233, 236, 237, 242, 247, 250, 252, 260, 266, 278, 280, 288, 289, 300, 305, 319, 321, 322.

American Military Government 101, 115, 148.
American Montessori Society 27.
Americanization 44.
Ames, David W. 188.
Amhara 209.
Amish 258.
Anauk 209.
Anderson, Jon 308.
Anglo-American 68.
Anthropological Quarterly 52.
Anthropological Society of London 10.
Anthropology Resource Center 298, 319.
Anthropometry 270.
Antiquities Act 26.
Aoki, T. 288.
Apache 280.
Applied Anthropology Unit 70.
Archeological and Historic Preservation Act 248.
Architecture 289.
Arctic Research Laboratory 176.
Arensberg, Conrad M. 81, 82, 95, 154.
Arizona State University 233.
Arvizu, Steven F. 239, 314.
Ashanti 43.
Ashley-Montagu, M. F. 162.
Attica Prison
Aurbach, Hervert A. 242.
Azande 167.
Baerreis, David A. 122.
Bailey, Wilfred C. 221.
Bainton, Barry R. 243, 291.
Balderston, F. E. 299.
Balikci, Asen 308.
Bank Street College of Education 238.
Banks, Dennis 247.
Bardach, John E. 194.
Barnett, Clifford R. 139, 232.
Barnett, Homer G. 128, 137, 141, 150, 201.
Barnett, Milton 139.
Barney, Ralph A. 181.
Barotse 102.
Barrett, Samuel A. 166.
Barrows, David P. 20, 22.
Bascom, William R. 121.
Basehart, Harry W. 202.
Bateson, Gregory 83.
Beaglehole, E. 125.

GENERAL INDEX

Beaglehole, P. 125.
Beals, Alan R. 155.
Beals, Ralph L. 90, 119, 122, 166.
Bell, Earl H. 80.
Bell, Robert E. 122.
Bellecourt, Clyde 247.
Belshaw, Cyril S. 249.
Beltran, Aguirre 171.
Benavides, Marisela 307.
Benedict, Burton 193.
Benedict, Ruth 87, 106.
Bennett, John W. 87, 115, 148.
Berg, Larry L. 233.
Bikini, Atomic Tests 142.
Bilingual 314, 321.
Bisset, Ronald 293.
Blasingham, Emily 122.
Board of Indian Commissioners 32.
Boas, Franz 33, 57.
Boggs, Stephan T. 164.
Boisvert, Richard 69.
Bomber Crews 155.
Boyer, Jefferson 303.
Breunig, Robert G. 250.
British Association for the Advancement of Science 46.
British Colonial Service 100.
Brokensha, David 211, 309.
Bromley, Yu. V. 36.
Brown, Esther Lucille 71.
Brown, G. Gordon 56, 66, 95, 146.
Brown vs. Board of Education 149.
Bryant, Carol A. 259.
Buchanan, Francis 4.
Buchsbaum, Herbert J. 81.
Buckles, Patricia K. 313.
Bureau of Agricultural Economics 82.
Bureau of American Ethnology 11, 19, 21, 28.
Bureau of Ethnic Research 266, 286.
Bureau of Indian Affairs 76, 94, 95, 139, 207, 300.
Bureau of Non-Christian Tribes 20.
Bureau of Reclamation 305.
Burns, Allan 276.
Cain, Stephen R. 225.
Caldwell, J. C. 271.
Calhoun, Craig Jackson 275.
California State University, Sacramento 239, 240, 314.
Callaway, Donald G. 278.

Cambridge University 23, 30.
Canfield, Robert 308.
Canter, Larry W. 315.
Cargo-cult 47.
Carley, Verna A. 187.
Carpenter, Edmund 67.
Carroll, Thomas 265.
Carroo, Agatha E. 259.
Cartter, Alan M. 299.
Caso, Alfonso 135.
Catholic Anthropological Conference 52.
Catholic University of America 52.
Census of India 206.
Center for Developmental Ghange 225.
Center for New Schools 294, 312.
Chambers, Erve 287, 315.
Chapman, Carl H. 122.
Chapman, K. 293.
Chapple, Eliot D. 81, 83, 146.
Charles III 3.
Chesky, Jane 94.
Cheyenne 261.
Chicanito Science Project 240.
Chilcott, John 242.
Chinantec 126.
Chinnery, W. P. 42, 45, 49.
Chiriboga, Carlos C. 168.
Choctaws 236.
Civil Affairs Handbooks 107.
Civil Works Administration 65.
Clark, B. D. 293.
Clark, Margaret 199.
Clark, Woodrow W. 294.
Clement, Dorothy C. 289.
Clinton, Charles A. 276, 315.
Clune, Francis J. 221.
Cochrane, Glyn 222, 253.
Cocopah 280.
Cohen, Fay G. 247.
Colbert, Billy K. 315.
Collier, John 95, 168.
Collier, Jr. John 242.
Collier, Mary 168.
Colombo Plan 158.
Colonial Administration 9, 15, 23, 37, 39, 40, 46, 48, 49, 50, 51, 54, 56, 59, 75, 86, 98, 100, 158, 196.

GENERAL INDEX

Colonial Development and Welfare Act 89.
Colonial Social Science Research Council 89, 108.
Comas, Juan 35, 144, 162.
Comitas, Lambros 208.
Commissioner of Indian Affairs 61.
Committee on Food Habits 87.
Committee on Human Relations in Industry 81.
Committee on National Morale 83.
Committee on Nursing and Anthropology 226.
Committee on Public Archeology 235.
Community Action Programs 225.
Community Advocacy 244.
Community Development 109, 138, 173, 187, 218, 231, 243, 282, 292.
Community Development Act 292.
Community Studies 79.
Conflict Resolution 273.
Conklin, Harold C. 195.
Conscientizacion 254.
Cook, S. F. 166.
Cooledge, Harold J. 128.
Cooperatives 217.
Coordinated Investigation of Micronesian Anthropology 128, 141.
Cordova, Andrew R. 92.
Cornell University 111, 139, 168, 171, 184, 218.
Cree 237.
Criswell, John H. 137, 176.
Cronk, Christine 270.
Cross-cultural Resource Center 314.
Cubans 259.
Cultural Resources Management 26, 248.
Cultural Therapy 174.
Culture-based Theory 189.
Culture Brokerage 165, 259.
Culture Shock 180.
Curriculum Development 201, 221, 239, 240, 251, 288.
Cushman, Frances 147.
Cutter, Donald 166.
Dalton, George 206.
D'Andrade, R. G. 299.
Davis, Allison 87.
Davis, Nancy Yaw 301.
Davis, R. N. 262.
Davis, Shelton 298, 319.
de Fuentes, Carmen 168.
deGarine, I. 304.
de la Fuente, Julio 136.

Dean, Linda Whileford 272.
Del Prado, Nuñez 198.
Deuscle, Kurt 184, 218.
Devonshire Training Scheme 100.
Dickson, W. J. 81.
Diesing, Paul 133.
Disaster Research 165.
Dixon, Mim 320.
Dobyns, Henry F. 122, 168.
Dorjahn, Vernon R. 208.
Doughty, Paul L. 168, 208.
Doukhobors 152.
Downing, Theodore 280, 286.
Down's Syndrome 270.
Driver, Harold 166.
Drucker, Philip 137, 150.
Drug Addiction 245.
DuBois, Cora 111.
Dumont, Jr., R. V. 212.
Duncan, J. T. 246.
Duncan, William 7.
Dupree, Louis 190, 208.
Dupree, Nancy 308.
Dyson-Hudson, N. 234.
Easley, Linda Elaine 279.
East India Company 4.
Ecafe 194.
Ecole Nationale de la France D'Outre-Mer 15.
Eddy, Elizabeth M. 6.
Edison, Thomas W. 279.
Education 34, 62, 66, 79, 86, 103, 123, 125, 131, 135, 174, 179, 201, 212,
    221, 224, 238, 242, 250, 251, 254, 258, 260, 265, 275, 288, 289, 294, 314.
Egeland, Janice A. 259.
Eggan, Fred 20, 22, 101.
Eiselein, E. B. 246.
Elkin, A. P. 120.
Ellis, Florence H. 122.
Elmendorf, Mary 313.
Elmendorf, William W. 122.
Elwin, Verrier 183, 192, 200, 203.
Embree, Edwin R. 62.
Embree, John F. 95, 101, 106, 115.
Employment 272, 299, 300.
Energy Resource Development 284, 285, 297.
Environmental Impact Statement 248.
Environmental Quality 257.
Epstein, A. L. 185.

GENERAL INDEX

Erasmus, Charles 157, 169.
Eskimo 176, 285, 300, 301.
Espinosa, Paul T. 314.
Ethics 146, 220, 249.
Ethnographic Observation 265.
Ethnohistory 261.
Ethnological Society of London 5.
Ethnographic Survey of India 25.
Ethnographic Survey of Ireland 18.
Ethnographic Survey of the United Kingdom 17.
Ethnosemantics 195, 241.
Euler, Robert C. 122.
Evans-Pritchard, E. E. 85.
Everhart, Robert B. 276.
Executive Order 11593 69.
Expert Witness 181.
Fabila, Alfonso 88.
Far Eastern Civil Affairs Training School 101.
Ferguson, Charles
Ferguson, Frances Northend 223.
Firth, Raymond 89, 158, 165.
Fisher, Burton R. 188.
Fisher, Margaret Welpley 70.
Fitting, James E. 65.
Fitzsimmons, Stephen J. 276.
Fletcher, Alice 14.
Follow Through Program 250.
Food and Agriculture Organization (FAO) 195, 304.
Ford Foundation 173, 246.
Forde, E. Daryll 24.
Foreign Assistance Act 283, 308.
Foreign Morale Analysis Division 106.
Foreign Service Institute 177.
Forjando Patria 35.
Fortes, Meyer 23, 34, 116.
Foster, George M. 3, 13, 71, 93, 157, 169, 187, 199, 210.
Fox Project 133.
Frank, Lawrence K. 83.
Freeland, J. B. 245.
Freeman, Milton M. R. 285.
Freid, Jacob 168.
Freire, Paulo 254.
Frerks, G. 307.
Fruitland Project 139.
Fuchs, Estelle 242.
Fuchs, Stephen 183.
Fulmer, Hugh 184.

Galla 209.
Gallaher, Jr., Art 225.
Gamio, Manuel 35, 53, 78.
Gardner, Burleigh B. 81, 110, 124.
Gardfield, Sidney 81.
Gearing, Fred 133, 265.
General Accounting Office 269.
General Allotment Act 14.
Ghost Dance Religion 16.
Gibson, Margaret A.
Gifford, Edward W. 166.
Gil, A. 314.
Gila River Indian Community 266.
Gilbert Islands 141.
Gladwin, Thomas 115, 164.
Gluckman, Max 75, 102, 114.
Golden Stool Incident 43.
Goldschmidt, Walter 155, 166.
Gomez, R. 246.
Goodenough, Ward H. 218.
Gorer, Geoffrey 99.
Gormley, Donald C. 181.
Great Lakes Inter-tribal Council 204.
Grosscup, Gordon L. 122.
Green, B. L. 262.
Grinstead, M. J. 262.
Gussow, Zachary 122.
Guthe, Carl 87.
Guzman de Velasco, Isabel 314.
Hackenberg, Robert A. 122.
Hadaway, Evelyn 191.
Haddon, A. C. 18.
Hailey, W. H. 41, 89, 196.
Hall, Edward T. 115, 121.
Halperin, Katherine Spencer 106.
Halpern, Abraham 70, 166.
Halpern, Joel 194.
Hamilton, James W. 164.
Hammel, E. A. 299.
Handbook of South American Indians 119.
Hansen, Asael T. 95, 161.
Hansen, William J. 308, 315.
Hanunoo 195.
Harding, Joe R. 289, 303.
Harper, Allan G. 92.
Harvey, Herbert R. 122.
Havasupai 280.

GENERAL INDEX

Havighurst, Robert J. 242.
Hawthorn, Harry B. 152.
Health Ecology Project 259.
Health Planning 105, 161, 169, 184, 209, 219.
Hearing Aid 303.
Heath, Dwight B. 208.
Hehe 56.
Heizer, Robert F. 122, 166.
Held, Jan 9.
Henderson, Eric 278.
Hester, James A. 122.
Highway Development 310.
Hines, Neal O. 277.
Hinsley, Curtis M., Jr. 16, 19, 21.
Historic American Building Survey 69.
Historic American Engineering Record 69.
Historic Sites Act 69.
Historic Sites Survey 69.
Hlady, Walter 237.
Hobbema Curriculum Project 288.
Hochstrasser, Donald L. 219.
Hodson, T. C. 23.
Hoebel, E. Adamson 179.

Hogbin, H. Ian 49, 60.
Holmberg, Allan R. 133, 168.
Homesteading 67.
Honigmann, John J. 175.
Horowitz, Irving Louis 220.
Horowitz, Michael M. 309.
Horsfall, Alexander 81.
Hostetler, John A. 258.
Housing 230, 231, 252, 264, 286, 287.
Howell, P. P. 98.
Hualapai 280.
Hudson's Bay Company 237.
Hughes, Wayne 265.
Huizer, Gerrit 136, 168.
Hulse, Frederick 106.
Human Organization 96, 146.
Human Services Delivery 297.
Human Waste Disposal 313.
Hunter, David E. 260.
Huntington, G. E. 258.
Husain, Tariq 234, 267.
Hutt, A. M. 56.
Hutton, J. H. 23.
Iaani, Francis A. J. 275.

Ibo 29.
Immigrants 53.
Impact Information Center 320.
INCAP 159.
India Village Service 109.
Indian Civil Service 23.
Indian Claims Commission 104, 118, 122, 166, 181.
Indian Community Action Program 233.
Indian Personality and Administration Project 94.
Indian Reorganization Act 70, 204.
Indians of California 104, 166.
Indirect Rule 29, 64.
Industrial Anthropology 42, 73, 81, 110, 262.
Ingersoll, Jasper 194.
Institute of Interamerican Affairs 169.
Institute of Social Anthropology 157.
Institute of Social Science Research 284.
Instituto Nacional Indigenista 126, 136, 140.
Inter Ethnic Relations 179.
Interamerican Indian Institute 78.
International Cooperation Administration 162.
International Institute of African Languages and Cultures 54, 75.
International Institute of Tropical Agriculture 227.
International Planned Parenthood Federation 193.
International Potato Center 256, 307.
IRSAC 129.
Isais, Raoul 314.
Ishino, Iwao 106, 148.
Jablow, Joseph 122.
Jacobs, Alan H. 317.
Jacobs, Sue-Ellen 274, 295, 305.
Jacobsen, Claire 238.
Jeffereys, M. D. W. 1, 2.
Jenks, Albert E. 20, 28, 44.
Jicarilla Apache 202.
Job Satisfaction 262.
Johnson, Norris Brock 294.
Joint Center for Urban Studies 214.
Jones, J. A. 181.
Jorgenson, Joseph 249.
Joseph, Alice 95.
Josselin de Jong, P. E. 40.
Kambatta 209.
Kariba Dam Project 229.
Kaufman, Howard K. 217.
Keiser, Lincoln 308.

GENERAL INDEX

Keith, Arthur 5.
Kelly, Isabel 157, 164, 169, 187.
Kelly, William H. 94.
Kennard, Edward A. 28, 76.
Kennedy, Donald A. 232.
Kennedy, John F. 205.
Kennedy, Raymond 9, 111.
Kern, M. Sue 215.
Kerri, James N. 264.
Kessing, Felix M. 67, 113.
Kickapoo 321.
Kidder, A. V. 118.
Kimball, Solon T. 68, 95, 161, 201.
Kimble, Robert 297.
Kiste, Robert C. 142, 277.
Kite, B. Alan 266.
Kluckhohn, Clyde 94, 106.
Kluger, Richard 149.
Knight, Margaret 242.
Kollmorgen, W. M. 80.
Kramer, Rita 27.
Kroeber, A. L. 122, 181.
Kuper, Adam 37, 38, 50, 55, 89, 108, 268.
Kuyo Chico Project 198.
LaBarre, Weston 156.
Lackner, Helen 29.
Laderman, Samuel 81.
Lake Powell Project 278.
Land Use 68, 114, 122, 301.
Landy, David 189.
Lantis, Margaret L. 191.
Lasswell, Harold D. 168.
Law 98, 102, 114.
Lear, John 168.
Lefley, Harriet P. 259.
Leighton, Alexander H. 95, 105, 106, 115, 139, 171.
Leighton, Dorothea C. 94, 105, 106.
Leininger, Madeline M. 226.
Leloup, Marcel 195.
Leonard, Olen 80.
Leroi-Gourhan, A. 15.
Lessa, William A. 128.
Levy, Jerrold E. 278.
Lewis, Kepler 177.
Lewis, Oscar 173.
Lindsay, A. J. 248.

Lipe, W. D. 248.
Little, Kenneth 201.
Loomis, Charles P. 80.
Loomis, Nellie H. 80.
Loumala, Katharine 95.
Low, J. O. 81.
Luckenbach, Alvin 69.
Lugard, F. D. 54.
Lurie, Nancy O. 14, 122, 204, 237.
Luzbetak, Louis J. 52.
McAllester, David P. 156.
McDaniel, C. K. 299.
McGee, W. J. 21.
McGimsey, Charles R. 26, 248.
MacGregor, Gordon 28, 70, 76, 79, 94, 97, 122, 147, 163, 177.
MacLiesh, Kenneth 80.
McNamara, Robert L. 178.
McNickle, D'Arcy 70.
McPherson, Laura 316.
Mahony, Frank J. 208.
Mair, Lucy P. 75, 112, 158, 196.
Majumdar, D. N. 25, 123.
Malinowski, Bronislaw 54.
Mandelbaum, David G. 201.
Manitoba Metis Federation 264.
Manners, Robert A. 122.
Mantaro Valley 307.
Maori 125.
Marbial Valley Project 127.
Maretzki, Thomas 208.
Maricopa 266.
Market Research 124.
Marriott, McKim 138.
Marshall Islands 141, 150.
Marshall, John F. 271.
Marshall, Wes 246.
Maruyama, Magorah 274, 296.
Masai 234, 317.
Mason, Leonard 121, 142.
Massachusetts Mental Health Center 189.
Mathews, Robert O. 298, 319.
Mathur, H. M. 200, 206.
Mauritius Family Planning Association 193.
Maybury-Lewis, David 322.
Mayer, Albert 138.
Mazatec 126.
Mead, Margaret 83, 87, 146, 186.

GENERAL INDEX

Media Anthropology 246.
Medical Anthropology 105, 169, 199, 318.
Meek, C. K. 41, 55.
MeKeel, H. Scudder 55.
Mekong River Project 194.
Menominees 188.
Mental Health 189, 244.
Mental Retardation 270.
Merolla da Sorrento, Jerome 2.
Merriam, C. Hart 104.
Messing, Simon D. 209.
Meti 237, 264.

Metraux, Alfred 127, 144.
Metraux, Rhoda 87.
Mexican-Americans 239, 246.
Mexican American Education Project 239.
Mexican Revolution 35.
Michaelson, Karen L. 310.
Michener, Bryan 242.
Miller, Elmer S. 52.
Miller, Merton L. 20.
Millsap, William 292.
Miner, Horace 82.
Miniclier, Louis 164, 187.
Minnesota Work Equity Program 311.
Missionary 1, 2, 7, 52, 109.
Missouri River 147.
Mitchell, J. Clyde 160.
Moe, E. O. 80.
Monge, Carlos 133, 168.
Montessori, Maria 27.
Montgomery, Edward 87.
Mooney, James 16.
Moore, David G. 110.
Moorehead, Warren K. 32.
Multipurpose Tribal Blocks 200.
Mumford, W. Bryant 62.
Murdock, George P. 107.
Murray, J. H. P. 45.
Mutual Self-Help 74.
Mwewa, Parkinson B. 185.
Myres, J. L. 12, 17, 29, 46.
Nadel, S. F. 77, 116.
Nader, Ralph 298.
Nag, Moni 213.
Nash, Philleo 205, 207.
National Aeronautics and Space Administration 296.

National Character 99.
National Environmental Policy Act 248, 274, 277, 292.
National Historic Preservation Act 69.
National Indian Youth Council 204.
National Institute of Education 294.
National Register of Historic Places 69.
National Research Council 57, 87.
National Science Foundation 310.
National Study of Indian Education 242.
Native American Church 156.
Navajo 94, 105, 139, 184, 223, 278, 289.
Naylor, Larry 300.
Nehru, Jawaharlal 192.
Nelleman, George 8.
Nesbitt, Paul H. 197.
Netting, Robert Mc. 133.
New Deal 68.
Newman, Marshall T. 168.
Nicaise, Joseph 41.
Nickerson, G. S. 219.
Niehoff, Arthur H. 154.
Nisbet, Robert A. 220.
Nishomoto, R. S. 91.
Nkrumah, Kwame 211.
Northeast Frontier Agency 183, 192.
Nuba 77.
Nursing 71, 215, 226.
Nutritional Anthropology 87.
Oberg, Kalervo 92, 157, 169, 180.
Office of Indian Affairs 72.
Office of War Information 106.
Officer, James E. 205.
Ogbu, John U. 314.
Oliver, Douglas T. 121.
Olson, Philip 80.
Omaha Allotment Act 14.
Ontiveros, Raymond A. 295.
Opler, Marvin K. 95.
Opler, Morris E. 55, 106.
Oxford University 13, 30.
Paiute 290.
Paoli, Lillian B. 294.
Pan American Health Organization 318.
Pan-Pacific Science Congress 49.
Papago 72, 94, 243, 252.
Papaloapan Resettlement Project 126.
Park, R. L. 138.

GENERAL INDEX

Participant-intervention 165.
Participant-observation 155, 190.
Partridge, William L. 6.
Passin, Herbert 87.
Patch, Richard W. 208.
Paul, Benjamin D. 201, 232.
Peace Corps 208, 228.
Pearsall, Marion 161, 215, 232.
Peattie, Lisa R. 133, 214, 230, 255, 281.
Pelzer, Karl 121.
Penncraft Resettlement Project 74.
Perham, Margery 58.
Peters, D. W. 114.
Peterson, John H. 236, 242, 315.
Peyote 156.
Philippine Ethnological Survey 28.
Phillips Academy 32.
Phoenix Indian School 79.
Piddington, Ralph 133.
Pima 266, 280.
Place Names 72.
Point IV Program 154.
Polgar, Steven 213, 216, 232, 271.
Popoloca 126.
Popular Magazine of Anthropology 10.
Population 193, 213, 216, 271.
Powdermaker, Hortense 87.
Powell, John Wesley 11, 21.
Precourt, Walter 265.
Prieto, A. G. 174.
Project Camelot 220.
Project Canada West 251.
Project Fiesta 246.
Project Headstart 238, 250.
Provinse, John H. 68, 82, 95.
Psychiatry 134.
Public Interest Anthropology 298.
Puerto Ricans 259.
Rabin, David L. 184.
Race 57, 144, 162.
Radcliffe-Brown, A. R. 34, 37, 60.
Radner, Roy 299.
Rapoport, Robert N. 201.
Rattray, W. S. 38, 43.
Ray, Verne 181.
Read, Margaret 86.
Recreational Planning 306.

Redfern, J. M. 262.
Redfield, Robert 82, 149.
Reining, Conrad C. 5, 10, 167.
Reining, Priscilla 267.
Research and Development Anthropology 168, 198, 244, 282, 290.
Resettlement 74, 211, 222, 227, 229.
Rhodes-Livingstone Institute 75, 102, 114, 160.
Rich, George W. 314.
Richards, A. I 42, 129.
Richards, Audrey 89.
Richards, Cara E. 184.
Richardson, Jr., F. L. W. 74.
Richardson, Sue E. 315.
Rink, Hinrich 8.
Rio Grande Socio-economic Survey 68.
Rios, Sam 240.
Risley, H. H. 24.
Roan Antelope Copper Mine 73.
Rockefeller Foundation 257.
Rodnick, David 70, 115.
Roethlisberger, F. J. 81.
Roosevelt, Theodore 32.
Rosenstiel, C. R. 245.
Royal Anthropological Institute 46.
Royal Irish Academy 18.
Royce, Charles C. 19.
Russell Sage Foundation 70, 171.
Russian Revolution 36.
Sabey, Ralph H. 251.
Sachchidananda 4.
Sahel 309.
Salamone, Frank J. 273.
Salisbury, Richard 263.
Sandoval, Mercedes C. 259.
Sangamon River 295.
Sanusi 117.
Sasaki, Tom T. 139, 202.
Schaedel, Richard P. 164.
Schaeffer, C. E. 70.
Schapera, Issac 64, 130.
Schensul, Stephen L. 244.
Schleicher, Barbara A. 295.
Schlesier, Karl 261.
School of Naval Administration 113.
Schoolcraft, Henry R. 6.
Schoorl, J. W. 182.

GENERAL INDEX

Scientific Investigations in Micronesia 141.
Scotch, Norman A. 232.
Scudder, Thayer 229, 309.
Sears Roebuck and Company 124.
Seijas, Haydee 271.
Seligman, G. C. 31.
Shahrani, Nazif 308.
Sharp, Lauriston 111.
Sheldon, R. C. 74.
Sherlock, Steven 294.
Sherman Indian School 79.
Shiloh, Ailon 228, 302.
Shriver, Sergeant 228.
Simmons, Ozzie 157, 169.
Simon, Margaret Sargent 62.
Singaribun, Masri 271.
Singh, Rudra Datt 138.
Sioux 97, 212.
Slotkin, J. S. 156.
Smith, Allen 265.
Smith, Edwin 59.
Smith, Elmer R. 179.
Smith, Harvey L. 87.
Smith, Robert J. 111.
Smithsonian Institution 157.
Smock, David P. 227.
Snyder, Warren 239, 314.
Social Impact Assessment 274, 284, 292, 293, 295, 305, 310, 315.
Social Network 272.
Social Research, Inc. 124.
Social Science Research Council 53, 57.
Social Soundness Analysis 283, 316.
Socialization 189, 258.
Society for American Archaeology 235.
Society for Applied Anthropology 93, 96, 146.
Society for Medical Anthropology 226, 232.
Society of Professional Anthropologists 291.
Soil Conservation Service 68, 76, 92.
Solenberger, R. R. 137.
Solheim, Wilhelm 194.
Solomon, R. Charles 315.
Somali 209.
Sorenson, John L. 233.
South Pacific Commission 132.
South Pacific Research Council 143.
Space Colonization 296.
Spanish-Americans 305.

University of Georgia 221.
University of Leiden 40.
University of London 86.
University of Minnesota 28, 44.
University of Montana 284.
University of Nebraska-Omaha 308.
University of South Dakota 97, 233.
University of Sydney 49, 51.
University of Texas 149.
University of Utah 233.
University Year for Action 260.
Union of Soviet Socialist Republics 36.
USSR Academy of Sciences 36.
Urban Planning 170, 214, 230, 279, 281.
Urbanization 160.
Useem, John 97, 121, 128, 137.
Useem, Ruth Hill 97.
Vailala Madness 47.
Van Tassell, Jon 310.
Van Vollenhoven, C. 64.
Van Willigen, John 243.
Varenne, Herve 275.
Vasquez, Mario C. 168.
Velimirovic, Boris 318.
Vicos 168, 198.
Villa-Rojas, Alfonso 126.
Vlachos, Evan 274, 315.
Voegelin, Erminie W. 122, 151, 166.
Voget, Fred W. 122.
Volta River Project 211.
Von Furer-Haimendorf, C. 103.
Wagina Resettlement Scheme 222.
Wallace, Anthony F. C. 16.
War Relocation Authority 91, 95.
Warner, W. Lloyd 81, 82, 124.
Wathern, P. 293.
Wax, Murray L. 212, 224, 250.
Wax, Rosalie H. 91, 212, 224.
Weaver, Thomas 266, 280, 286.
Weidman, Hazel H. 232, 259.
Welfare Reform 311.
Weltfish, Gene 118.
Weppner, Robert S. 245.
Werge, Robert W. 256, 307.
Western Carolines 141.
Western Electric 81.
White, Paul E. 232.

GENERAL INDEX

Toilet Training 99.
Tonga, 114.
Tothill, J. D. 167.
Tozo, Leon 259.
Train, Percy 122.
Training in Applied Anthropology 201.
Trans-Alaska Pipeline 300, 320.
Trapnell, C. G. 114.
Truman, Harry S. 207.
Trend, M. G. 311.
Tuamotus 141.
Tuberculosis Eradication 219.
Tucson Garbage Research Project 269.
Turner, Allen C. 290.
Tylor, E. B. 13.
Uhlman, Julie M. 297.
Ujamaa 267.
Underhill, Ruth 72.
UNESCO 127, 144, 162, 186.
U. S. Air Force 155, 190, 197.
U. S. Army Corps of Engineers 274, 295, 315.
U. S. Army Engineer Waterways Experiment Station 315.
U. S. Commissioner of Indian Affairs 207.
U. S. Commercial Company 121.
U. S. Congress 6, 319.
U. S. Department of Agriculture 68, 76, 80, 82, 92.
U. S. Department of Defense 277.
U. S. Department of Housing and Urban Development 252, 280, 287.
U. S. Department of the Interior 153.
U. S. Department of Justice 181.
U. S. Department of Labor 272, 311.
U. S. Department of the Navy 106, 128, 131, 137, 141, 150, 153, 176.
U. S. Department of State 106, 111, 119, 151, 175.
U. S. Department of War 106.
U. S. Immigration Commission 33.
U. S. Office of Economic Opportunity 225, 233, 238.
U. S. Office of Education 221, 224, 239, 265, 276.
U. S. Office of Indian Affairs 97.
U. S. Public Health Service 191, 252, 286, 303.
United States Supreme Court 149, 258.
Universal Declaration of Human Rights 145.
University of Aberdeen 293.
University of Alabama 161.
University of Arizona 269, 286.
University of California 91.
University of California, Berkeley 201.
University of Chicago 101.

Spearpoint, F. 73.
Spicer, Edward H. 35, 61, 82, 84, 95, 171, 205, 231.
Spicer, Rosamond B. 94.
Spillius, James 165.
Spindler, George 174.
Spoehr, A. 128.
Spradley, James 241.
Srb, Jozetta 96.
Stanford University 113.
Starch, Elmer A. 187.
State University of New York-Buffalo 265.
Sterner, Armin 79.
Steward, Julian H. 70, 119, 122, 166, 181.
Stewart, Omer C. 32, 104, 118, 156, 166.
Stirling, Gene 70.
Stocking, George W., Jr. 33, 57.
Stout, David B. 122.
Strong, W. M. 45.
Strong, William D. 166.
Student Mobilization Committee to End the War in Vietnam 249.
Stull, Donald D. 321.
Survival Training 190.
Swadesh, Maurice 84.
Sweatt v Painter 149.
Swidden Agriculture 195.
Sylvain, Jeanne G. 127.
Szanton, David L. 208.
Taft, William Howard 22.
Tarascan 84.
Tax, Sol 133, 156, 170, 204.
Taylor, Carl C. 80, 82.
Taylor, Herbert C. 122.
Taylor, Paul S. 187.
Technical Cooperation-Bureau of Indian Affairs 72, 76.
Temple, Richard 23.
Tensas River Valley 315.
Tepalcatepec Basin Project 172.
Termination 188.
Textor, Robert B. 148, 208, 228.
Therapeutic Anthropology 302.
Thomas, D. S. 91.
Thomas, W. Northcote 29.
Thompson, Laura 70, 94, 201.
Throgmorton, David 297.
Tigre 209.
Tindall, B. Allan 265.
Tobin, Jack A. 277.

GEOGRAPHICAL INDEX

Africa 108, 196.
American Samoa 113, 163.
Americas 78.
Andaman Islands 123.
Australia 112, 121.
Bechuanaland 63, 130.
Belgium 29, 129.
Brazil 157, 169, 180, 254.
British Solomons 165, 222.
Cambodia 194
Canada 152, 237, 251, 264, 285, 288.
Cape Colony 12.
Chile 169, 220.
Colombia 157, 169.
Congo 2, 129.
Denmark 8.
East Africa 59.
Ecuador 169, 281.
Egypt 30, 187.
El Salvador 169.
Ethiopia 209.
France 15, 54, 144, 145, 162.
Guatemala 159.
Germany 115.
Ghana 211.
Gold Coast 38, 43, 187.
Great Britain 1, 5, 10, 13, 17, 23, 30, 46, 60, 75, 86, 89, 100, 108, 158, 293.
Greenland 8.
Guam 113.
Haiti 127.
India 4, 25, 103, 109, 123, 135, 138, 173, 183, 187, 192, 200, 203, 206.
Ireland 18.

GENERAL INDEX

Whitefore, Andrew H. 81.
Whitten, Phillip 260.
Whyte, William F. 65, 158, 198.
Willamette Valley 257.
Willard, William 231.
Williams, F. E. 45, 47, 48.
Williams, Michael Ronan 279.
Wilson, Godfrey 75.
Wilson, M. L. 82.
Wilson, Stephen 312.
Wingate, Reginald 30.
Winnebago 204.
Wisdom, Charles 70.
Wiser, William H. 109.
Witchcraft 182.
Wolf, Eric 249.
Wolfe, Alvin W. 272, 302.
Wolfe, Leo J. 202.
Wollamo 209.
Works Progress Administration 65.
World Bank 234, 253, 267, 313.
World Health Organization 271.
Wright, E. F. 81.
Wulff, Robert M. 252, 282, 306.
Wynne, Waller 80.
Wyoming Human Services Project 297.
Yaqui 88.
Young, Hubert 75.
Young, John A. 257.
Young, Kimball 80.
Zambezi Basin 229.
Zande Scheme 167.
Zuni 94.

Italy 26, 54.
Jamaica 268.
Japan 99, 101, 106, 107, 113, 115, 148.
Kenya 234.
Laos 194.
Lebanon 177.
Libya 116, 117.
Mauritius 193.
Mexico 35, 78, 84, 126, 136, 140, 159, 169, 172.
Micronesia 121, 128, 137, 141, 142, 150, 153, 277.
Morocco 304.
Netherlands 9, 40, 64, 182.
Netherlands East Indies 9, 62
New Guinea 42, 45, 47, 48, 49, 51, 112, 120, 182, 263.
New Zealand 125.
Nigeria 29, 41, 55, 58, 227.
Northern Rhodesia 75, 102, 114, 160, 185.
Oceania 107, 115.
Pakistan 175, 187.
Paraguay 322.
Peru 157, 168, 169, 198, 256, 307.
Philippines 20, 22, 28, 187, 195.
Ruanda-Urundi 129.
Sierra Leone 29.
South Africa 24, 37, 50, 54.
Southeast Asia 178, 111, 194.
Spain 3.
Sudan 30, 31, 77, 85, 98, 167.
Switzerland 271.
Tanganyika/Tanzania 56, 267, 317.
Thailand 194, 249.
Tonga 34.
United Nations 186.
United States 6, 7, 11, 14, 16, 19 21, 26, 32, 33, 44, 52, 53, 57, 61, 65, 66, 67, 68, 69, 70, 71, 72, 74, 76, 79, 80, 82, 83, 87, 90, 91, 92, 93, 94, 95, 96, 97, 99, 101, 104, 105, 106, 110, 111, 113, 115, 118, 119, 122, 124, 131, 132, 133, 134, 139, 143, 146, 147, 149, 151, 154, 155, 156, 157, 161, 164, 166, 169, 170, 171, 174, 176, 177, 178, 179, 180, 181, 184, 187, 188, 189, 190, 191, 197, 199, 201, 202, 204, 205, 207, 208, 210, 212, 213, 215, 216, 218, 219, 220, 221, 223, 224, 225, 226, 228, 230, 231, 232, 235, 236, 238, 239, 240, 241, 242, 243, 244, 245, 246, 247, 248, 250, 252, 253, 255, 257, 258, 259, 260, 261, 262, 265, 266, 269, 270, 272, 273, 274, 275, 276, 278, 279, 280, 282, 283, 284, 286, 287, 289, 290, 291, 292, 294, 295, 296, 297, 298, 299, 300, 301, 302, 303, 305, 306, 308, 309, 310, 311, 312, 312, 314, 315, 316, 318, 319, 320, 321.
Venezuela 214.
Viet-Nam 194, 217.
Zambia 229.